EARTHEN Vessels

Devotional Thoughts from the Best of J. Oswald Sanders

Compiled by James Stuart Bell

Discovery House Publishers

Books, music, and videos that feed the soul with the Word of God

Box 3566 Grand Rapids, MI 49501

Discovery House Publishers is affiliated with RBC Ministries, Grand Rapids, Michigan.

Discovery House books are distributed to the trade exclusively by Barbour Publishing, Inc., Uhrichsville, Ohio.

Requests for permission to quote from this book should be directed to: Permissions Department, Discovery House Publishers, P O Box 3566, Grand Rapids, MI 49501.

Unless otherwise indicated, Scripture quotations are from the New International Version® ©1973, 1978, 1984 by International Bible Society. Used by permission of Zondervan. All rights reserved.

Material taken from *Spiritual Maturity* by J. Oswald Sanders ©1980. Used by permission of Moody Publishers, Chicago, IL. All rights reserved.

Material taken from *Spiritual Leadership* by J. Oswald Sanders © 1980. Used by permission of Moody Publishers, Chicago, IL. All rights reserved.

Material taken from *Spiritual Discipleship* by J. Oswald Sanders ©1989. Used by permission of Moody Publishers, Chicago, IL. All rights reserved.

Material taken from *The Incomparable Christ* by J. Oswald Sanders ©1970. Used by permission of Moody Publishers, Chicago, IL. All rights reserved.

Design and typesetting by Lakeside Design Plus

Library of Congress Cataloging-in-Publication Data

Sanders, J. Oswald (John Oswald), 1902–
    Earthen vessels : devotional thoughts from the best of J. Oswald
Sanders / compiled by James Bell.
        p. cm.
    ISBN 1-57293-160-4
    1. Bible—Devotional literature. I. Bell, James S. II. Title.
    BS491.5.S26 2006
    242—dc22

                                                    2005028236

Printed in the United States of America
05 06 07 08 09 10 / /10 9 8 7 6 5 4 3 2 1

Contents

Introduction	11	Dealing with Jealousy	55
The Spirit Helps Us	15	No Double Standard	57
Heaven's Many Mansions	17	Loyalty to the Master	59
In the Father's Hands	19	Cleansing by the Blood	61
God-Given Interruptions	21	The Sacrifice of Christ	63
Loneliness in Leadership	23	The Indwelling of Christ	65
Molding Character	25	The Satanic World System	67
Praying for Rulers	27	Imitating Christ	69
A Reshaped Ambition	29	Acceptable Worship	71
The Force of Self-Discipline	31	Comfort to Comfort Others	73
Spiritual Wisdom	33	Weakness and Strength	75
The Lordship of Christ	35	God Behind the Scenes	77
The Question of Church Discipline	37	The Inner Circle	79
Remaining in Front	39	The Joy of Friendship	81
Interceding for Missionaries	41	The World Hates the Church	83
Inward Renewal	43	The Law of Love	85
Nehemiah's Leadership Objectives	45	Intimacy through Growing Love	87
The Slowness of God	47	Simple Obedience	89
The Greatest Is Love	49	Focus on the Eternal	91
The Need to Evangelize	51	True Greatness	93
Love Is Patient and Kind	53	Natural Leadership Qualities	95

More Leadership Qualities 97

Do You Qualify to Lead? 99

The Likeness of Christ 101

The Call to Courage 103

A Leader's Humility 105

An Angry Leader 107

The Ape of God 109

Slaves Set Free 111

Responsibility for the
Lost 113

Dealing with Doubt 115

The Need for Patience 117

A Purpose for Each Life 119

Ways to Worship 121

Spiritual Gifts 123

The Judge Is Judged 125

The Value of Prohibitions 127

Christ in Paul 129

The Breath of God 131

Tests of Spiritual
Authority 133

Moral Perfection 135

Seek Counsel 137

The Humble Carpenter 139

Our Resurrection Bodies 141

Prayer and the Will of
God 143

Retirement Opportunities 145

The Location of Heaven 147

Responsibility to Witness 149

The Passover Song 151

Rich Yet Poor 153

Yes and Amen 155

Prayer and Predestination 157

Growing in Wisdom 159

Time and Eternity 161

Paul's Thorn 163

Warfare and Weapons 165

The Model Prayer 167

The Supremacy of Love 169

The Gift of the Spirit 171

Valuable Vessels 173

Faith and Sight 175

Doors of Opportunity 177

Ups and Downs of
Leadership 179

Seen and Unseen 181

Preparation for Ministry 183

Death Is Not Final 185

Human in Every Sense 187

The Cure for Loneliness 189

Reaping the
Consequences 191

The Perils of Leadership 193

The Weak Conscience 195

The Fire of God 197

If in Doubt . . . Question 199

God-Given Time 201

6

Prayer and Conscience	203	Lordship Salvation	255
I Must Choose	205	Imperfect Leaders	257
The Law of Restraint	207	Sharing God's Glory	259
God's Enabling Power	209	The Senior Partner	261
Responding in Service	211	Paul's Great Ambition	263
The True Vine	213	Extravagant Service	265
Restoring Relationships	215	A Strong Devotional Life	267
Never Give Up	217	Unanswered Prayer	269
Forms of Pride	219	Money: A Test of Character	271
Joy of Tithing	221		
God's Veto	223	The Living One	273
Supernatural Resources	225	Never Alone	275
Giving Beyond the Limit	227	The Potter and the Clay	277
Necessity for Preparation	229	Signs of Christ's Return	279
Midlife Stamina	231	Learning New Skills	281
Ascension into Heaven	233	Consecrated for Service	283
A Vision of God and Oneself	235	The Purpose of Life	285
Ignorance and Forgiveness	237	Husbands and Wives	287
The Art of Prayer	239	The Sacrifice of Intercession	289
Genuine Humility	241		
Fear Him Who Destroys	243	Christ's Victory over Satan	291
Instruction for Converts	245	The Realm of Satan	293
Interceding for the Lost	247	The Pitfalls of Popularity	295
The Meaning of Meekness	249	Answers to Temptation	297
God Carries on the Work	251	Supporting Subordinates	299
Proclaiming the Kingdom	253	He Is Without Sin	301

Nehemiah the Model
Leader   303
The Greatest Teacher   305
Humility as a Primary
Virtue   307
Who Is on Trial?   309
Aspects of the Atonement   311
Mysterious Darkness   313
Final Justice   315
The Time of His Coming   317
Thankfulness   319
Pleading the Promises   321
Life in Heaven   323

Should We Fast?   325
Redeem the Time   327
Rewards in Heaven   329
Prayer and Revival   331
Life Is a Tapestry   333
Greater Fruitfulness   335
He Is Worthy   337
The Wick's Oil   339
God Controls
Circumstances   341
Steps in Discerning God's
Will   343
The Lamb's Book of Life   345

List of Abbreviations

The selections in this volume have been compiled from over half of J. Oswald Sanders's titles. For those readers who wish to delve more deeply into the writings of Sanders, we have provided an abbreviation of the title of the source from which each selection was taken. The following is a list of those abbreviations and their corresponding titles.

31 Days	*31 Days on the Life of Christ;* also *The Incomparable Christ*
BB	*The Best That I Can Be*
BF	*Bible Men of Faith;* also *Robust in Faith*
CC	*Cameos of Comfort*
DA	*Divine Art of Soul Winning*
EI	*Enjoying Intimacy with God*
EL	*Every Life Is a Plan of God*
EY	*Enjoying Your Best Years*
FL	*Facing Loneliness*
HB	*Heaven: Better by Far*
HL	*How Lost Are the Heathen*
JL	*Just Like Us;* also *People Just Like Us*
PL	*Paul the Leader;* also *Dynamic Spiritual Leadership*
PLL	*Promised Land Living;* also *Christian's Promised Land*
PP	*Prayer Power Unlimited*
SC	*A Spiritual Clinic;* also *Problems of Christian Discipleship*

SD   *Spiritual Discipleship;* also *Shoe Leather Commitment, The Joy of Following Jesus*

SL   *Spiritual Leadership;* also *Guidelines for Disciples*

SM   *Spiritual Maturity;* also *On to Maturity*

SN   *Satan Is No Myth*

SP   *Spiritual Problems;* also *Spiritual Lessons*

Introduction

J. Oswald Sanders was an international Christian preacher, missionary statesman, prolific author, and gifted administrator who went to be with the Lord on October 24, 1992. He is primarily remembered for his Christian classic *Spiritual Leadership*, which continues to be widely distributed. This book still has a major impact on Christian leaders, both prominent and little known, around the world. Some, including Charles Colson, call it the best volume on spiritual leadership ever written.

As with many servants of God who were faithful to Him in past generations, memories begin to fade with the rise of the next generation of leaders. Their exploits in the cause of Christ and their written works are largely forgotten, unless they are among the "superstars" of the likes of a Moody or a Spurgeon. This could have happened in the next decade with the works of J. Oswald Sanders. In today's publishing environment it is difficult to keep even good "backlist" titles in print to compete with the latest spiritual fad.

Therefore, it has been my joy and privilege to compile and update a selection of the writings of Sanders, whom I consider to be a spiritual giant with an extraordinary knowledge of the Word and a total commitment to Christ. His writings continue to speak profoundly to our contemporary situation, and in these selections drawn from his many books, I bring to the reader a wide variety of his teaching and exhortation on numerous spiritual topics. Sanders wrote on many topics that are contained in this volume, including prayer, guidance, evangelism, heaven, and loneliness. The main focus and strength of Sanders, however, is on both leadership and discipleship. This material is largely found in three titles still in print: *Spiritual Leadership*, *Spiritual Discipleship*, and *Spiritual Maturity*.

Before you begin reading, let me share a brief biographical sketch. J. Oswald Sanders's passion was to train those who were called to serving Christ full-time on the mission field, but his journey did not begin there. J.O., as he was known, was the third child of Alfred and Margaret Sanders, immigrants to New Zealand from the United Kingdom. He studied law, which he practiced briefly, but his life was profoundly impacted at convention meetings in 1921 when he responded to the call to dedicate his life to serve on the mission field.

J. O. began in an administrative post with the China Inland Mission and eventually held key positions in the Bible College of New Zealand and other Christian organizations. He also became the editor of *The Reaper*, the country's largest interdenominational magazine. Yet he was much better known as a writer of books. His first book on evangelism, *The Divine Art of Soul Winning*, was published in 1937. It was the first of over forty titles that he would publish during his lifetime. His final book, *Enjoying Your Best Years*, focused on ways we can serve the Lord more fully in our later years—a lesson that he modeled by his continuing service.

In 1954 he became the fifth general director of the China Inland Mission, now renamed the Overseas Missionary Fellowship. In 1980 he was given an Order of the British Empire award in honor of his work with the New Zealand Bible College, and in 1992 an honorary doctorate in theology on the seventieth anniversary of the college.

My hope is that in regular reading of these representative selections of the finest of his writing, you will grow not only in spiritual leadership but in every facet of the Christian life that this book has to offer.

James Stuart Bell

The Spirit Helps Us

The Spirit Himself leads us into the presence of the Father. "For through him we . . . have access to the Father by one Spirit" (Ephesians 2:18). The picture behind *access* is that of a court official introducing people who desire an audience with the king. This is exactly what the Spirit does for us.

As the "spirit of grace and supplication" (Zechariah 12:10), He overcomes our reluctance, working in us the desire to pray. He graciously, yet faithfully, reveals to us our true heart-needs, and He leads us to seek their fulfillment in prayer.

He imparts an assurance in worship and a receptivity that creates freedom and confidence in the presence of God. "God sent the Spirit of his Son into our hearts, the Spirit who calls out, '*Abba* Father'" (Galatians 4:6). Children are uninhibited in the presence of an understanding and loving father, and so may we be in our prayers to our heavenly Father.

He helps us in the ignorance of our minds and in the weakness of our bodies, as well as in the sickness of the soul. "In the same way, the Spirit helps us in our weakness. We do not know what we ought to pray for" (Romans

8:26), or as it is in the King James Version, "We know not what we should pray for as we ought."

We can count on the Spirit's aid in guiding us into the will of God by illuminating Scripture to us and by stimulating and directing our mental processes. He purifies our desires and redirects them toward the will of God, for He alone knows and can interpret God's will and purpose. "No one knows the thoughts of God except the Spirit of God" (1 Corinthians 2:11). He also increases our motivation and inspires confidence and faith in a loving Father. *(PP)*

Heaven's Many Mansions

The Christian concept of heaven far outstrips Jewish thought. It is immeasurably higher and more detailed than Old Testament speculations. As Alexander Maclaren put it, heaven is a place of indescribable splendor, of blessedness and peace. We are left by its biblical description with an image of a life that will far transcend anything we have known so far. So incredibly glorious is it, that we are compelled to express it in both negative terms and by symbols of grandeur and majesty, "gathered," as Maclaren said, "from what is noblest and best in human building and society."

But what makes heaven what it is for the Christian is the perpetual presence of God as sovereign ruler of the universe and yet at the same time as our loving heavenly Father, and the reality of enjoying forever the companionship of our Redeemer and Lord. "Now the dwelling of God is with men, and he will live with them. They will be his people, and God himself will be with them and be their God" (Revelation 21:3).

Will mansions be awaiting us? "In my Father's house are many mansions: if it were not so, I would have told you. I go to prepare a place for you. And if I go and prepare a place for you, I will come again, and receive you unto myself; that where I am, there ye may be also" (John 14:2–3 KJV).

These treasured words have imparted more comfort to dying saints and grieving relatives than any other portion of Scripture. Scottish writer Ian Maclaren [not to be confused with Alexander above] gave this testimony: "Whenever I am called to a house of sickness or sorrow, I always read to the troubled folk John 14. Nothing else is so effective. If a man is sinking into unconsciousness, and you read about many mansions, he will come back and whisper 'mansions,' and will wait until you finish—'that where I am, there you may be also.'" Ian Maclaren lived in a day when people were familiar enough with the Scriptures to finish the sentence, but today not all would recognize the allusion.

"Trust me!" our Lord urged His followers. He spoke these words on the night before the cross to His dearly loved disciples, who were devastated at the thought of His leaving them. So He encouraged them to keep on trusting Him. *(HL)*

In the Father's Hands

We can be assured that we will receive all that God is willing to consistently grant us when we have prayed the prayer of faith in accordance with Mark 11:24. We can rest assured that He will exercise His divine influence on those who are the subjects of our prayers. He will do this to the fullest possible extent, short of encroaching on their free wills, so as to enable them to come to Christ or to otherwise conform to His will. We can be sure that He will choose the best time and employ the best methods to make His influence felt.

But what if the prayer does not seem to be answered, in spite of the sincerity of our desires and the earnestness of our pleas? Some light is thrown on our perplexity by the fact that our Lord Himself had to face the same problem. He did not see His heart's desire for humanity realized in every case. There were those over whom He had to utter the lament of unfulfilled love: "O Jerusalem, Jerusalem . . . how often I have longed to gather your children together, as a hen gathers her chicks under her wings, but you were not willing!" (Luke 13:34). And on another occasion He had to mourn, "You refuse to come to me to have life" (John 5:40).

19

No accusation about failure in prayer or about lack of true concern for the people being prayed for could be laid at His door, as it can all too often be laid at ours. But in spite of this, sometimes His prayers were not answered immediately or in the way we would expect. Yet He refused to exercise His divine power in order to compel people to come to Him. This is what is involved in the solemn responsibility of being human. We can say no to God.

However, this did not discourage Jesus from praying. He recognized the solemn fact, as we must, that in the final analysis the human will can become so debased that it can thwart the loving desires of God's heart. In the face of those circumstances, He did what we must do. He prayed and trustingly left the issue in the hands of His Father. *(PP)*

God-Given Interruptions

How interesting that the gospel accounts contain no hint of any interruption disturbing the serenity of the Son of God. Few things are more likely to produce tension in a busy life than unexpected interruptions. Yet to Jesus there were no such things. "Unexpected" events were always foreseen in the Father's planning, and Jesus was therefore undisturbed by them. True, at times there was hardly time to eat, but time was always sufficient to accomplish all the Father's will.

The pressure a spiritual leader feels often comes from assuming tasks that God has not assigned; for such tasks the leader cannot expect God to supply the extra strength required.

One busy man told me how he mastered the problem of interruptions. "Up to some years ago," he testified, "I was always annoyed by them, which was really a form of selfishness on my part. People used to walk in and say, 'Well, I just had two hours to kill here in between trains, and I thought I would come and see you.' That used to bother me. Then the Lord convinced me that He sends people our way. He sent Philip to the Ethiopian eunuch.

21

He sent Barnabas to see Saul. The same applies today. God sends people our way.

"So when someone comes in, I say, 'The Lord must have brought you here. Let us find out why He sent you. Let us have prayer.' Well, this does two things. The meeting takes on new importance because God is in it. And it generally shortens the meeting. If a visitor knows you are looking for reasons why God should have brought him, and there are none apparent, the visit becomes pleasant but brief.

"So now I take interruptions as from the Lord. They belong in my schedule, because the schedule is God's to arrange at His pleasure."

Paul affirms that God has a plan for every life. We have been "created in Christ Jesus to do good works, which God prepared in advance for us to do" (Ephesians 2:10). Through daily prayer, the leader discovers the details of that plan and arranges work accordingly. Each half-hour should have its own purpose, and we should make use of each one. *(SL)*

Loneliness in Leadership

In every leadership position, crises will arise sooner or later when the burden of responsibility seems far beyond our ability to bear it. Paul found himself in such a position when ministering in the province of Asia.

"We were under great pressure, far beyond our ability to endure, so that we despaired even of life. Indeed, in our hearts we felt the sentence of death" (2 Corinthians 1:8). But the God in whom he trusted carried him through.

From its very nature the role of a leader must be a rather lonely one, for leaders must always be ahead of their followers in some areas. Though many leaders are the most friendly and outgoing of people, inevitably there will be some paths they must be prepared to tread alone. It was the German philosopher Nietzsche's contention that life always gets harder near the summit—the cold increases and the path becomes more difficult. Mountain climbers affirm the truth that "the higher you go, the lonelier it gets."

Dixon E. Hoste, one member of a renowned missionary team, "The Cambridge Seven," profoundly understood this truth when Hudson Taylor, founder of the China Inland Mission, passed the reins of leadership into his hands. The China Inland Mission was the first of the so-called "Faith Missions," and it was at that time the largest.

After the momentous interview during which the frail leader passed on the torch to his successor, Hoste, deeply moved and aware of the weight of responsibility that now rested on his shoulders, said to himself, "And now I have no one but God."

Human nature craves companionship, and it is a natural desire for a leader to want to share with others the burdens of responsibility, especially when decisions of far-reaching consequence must be made. It is heartbreaking at times for a leader to have to make adverse decisions affecting the future of loved colleagues—and make them alone. This is one of the costliest aspects of leadership, but sometimes the price must be paid if one's leadership is to be productive. *(FL)*

Molding Character

ake pains with these things; be absorbed in them, so that your progress will be evident to all" (1 Timothy 4:15–16 NASB). Lesslie Newbigin goes so far as to question whether the church ought to encourage the concept of leadership, so difficult it is to use without being misled by its non-Christian counterpart. The church needs saints and servants, not "leaders," and if we forget the priority of service, the entire idea of leadership training becomes dangerous. Leadership training must still follow the pattern our Lord used with His Twelve.

Perhaps the more strategic and fruitful work of Christian workers is to help leaders of tomorrow develop their spiritual potential. This task requires careful thought, wise planning, endless patience, and genuine Christian love. It cannot be haphazard or ill conceived. Our Lord devoted the greater part of His three years of ministry to molding the characters and spirits of His disciples.

Paul showed the same concern for training young Timothy and Titus. Paul's method for preparing Timothy for the church in Ephesus is deeply instructive.

Timothy was about twenty years old when Paul became his friend. Timothy tended toward despondency, and he was too tolerant of and partial to people of rank. He could be irritable with opponents. He was apt to rely on old spiritual experiences rather than kindle the flame of daily devotion.

But Paul had high hopes for him. Paul set about to correct Timothy's timid nature, to replace softness with steel. Paul led Timothy into experiences and hardships that toughened his character. Paul did not hesitate to assign him tasks beyond his present powers. How else can a young person develop competence and confidence if not by stretching to try the impossible?

Traveling with Paul brought Timothy into contact with men of stature whose characters kindled in him a wholesome ambition to serve Christ. He learned from his mentor to triumphantly meet the crises that Paul considered routine. Paul shared with Timothy the work of preaching. Paul gave him the responsibility of establishing a group of Christians at Thessalonica. Paul's exacting standards, high expectations, and heavy demands brought out the best in Timothy, saving him from a life of mediocrity as a leader. *(SL)*

Praying for Rulers

"I urge . . . that requests, prayers, intercession and thanksgiving be made for everyone—for kings and all those in authority, that we may live peaceful and quiet lives in all godliness and holiness" (1 Timothy 2:1–2). Christians have civic and national as well as spiritual responsibilities, and, among other ways, we are to discharge these responsibilities in prayer. We should pray for those who hold civic office and national or international offices on all levels. Are we discharging our responsibilities in this area? Is it any wonder that the voice of the church is so muted and her influence so minimal in the affairs of the world when she neglects this primary and divinely ordained method of influencing national and world affairs? If prayer cannot influence the course of world events, Paul's exhortation is pointless.

Scripture teaches that the church and the Christian owe a duty to the state beyond mere payment of taxes and obedience to laws. It matters not whether rulers are good or bad; we are under obligation to pray for them as they exercise their offices. It is instructive to note that the ruler in Rome when Paul penned this letter to Timothy was the

27

infamous Nero. Rulers may be persecutors or dictators, but Christians are not to stop praying for them.

In general, the early Christians did not evade or ignore their divinely imposed civic and national responsibilities. One of the early Fathers, Tertullian, gives us a glimpse into their practice: "We pray for ourselves, for the state of the world, for the peace of all things, and for the postponement of the end."

Public officials have heavy burdens to bear, and they wield far-reaching influence. Their decisions affect the church, the city, and the nation. We must realize that the deeds of wicked people and corrupt officials can be held in check by our prayers.

In the midst of toppling thrones, Daniel maintained his serenity because he knew there was a sovereign God in heaven to whom he could pray. For him, that canceled every adverse factor. He could defy the decree of the ruler of Babylon, for he knew that "the Most High is sovereign over the kingdoms of men and gives them to anyone he wishes" (Daniel 4:17). *(PP)*

A Reshaped Ambition

A leader is usually an ambitious person. Even in his unregenerate days, the apostle Paul had been fiercely ambitious, and conversion certainly did not quench that flame. He could not do things halfway, for there seemed to be an inner compulsion that drove him relentlessly forward. Impatient of the status quo, his gaze was always trained on greater achievements and distant horizons.

Paul's unregenerate ambition had previously focused on refuting the teachings of the impostor Jesus, exterminating His followers and quenching the growing influence of His church. His burning zeal for Judaism, which he considered the only true religion, drove him to wild excesses. Until the time of his dramatic conversion, "Saul was still breathing out murderous threats against the Lord's disciples" (Acts 9:1).

On several occasions Paul told of the hardened state of his heart before conversion: "I persecuted the followers of this Way to their death, arresting both men and women and throwing them into prison" (Acts 22:4). "Many a time I went from one synagogue to another to have them punished, and I tried to force them to blaspheme. In my obsession against them, I even went to foreign cities to persecute them" (Acts 26:11). "I was advancing in Judaism beyond many Jews of my own age and was extremely zealous for the traditions of my fathers" (Galatians 1:14). These were the actions of an overzealous man.

The providence of God is further seen in the way this intense natural ambition was redirected into spiritually productive channels diametrically opposed to those of former days. His new ambition found a fresh center in the glory of Christ and the advancement of His kingdom. Paul nailed his old ambition to the cross, now longing to bring blessing to those whose extermination he had once plotted. "I long to see you," he wrote to the believers in Rome, "so that I may impart to you some spiritual gift to make you strong" (Romans 1:11). *(PL)*

The Force of Self-Discipline

eaders are able to lead others only because they discipline themselves. The person who does not know how to bow to discipline imposed from without, who does not know how to obey, will not make a good leader—nor will the one who has not learned to impose discipline within his or her own life. Those who scorn scripturally or legally constituted authority or rebel against it rarely qualify for high leadership positions.

Paul imposed on himself a rigorous inner discipline in two areas:

He waged war with his body. "I do not run like a man running aimlessly; I do not fight like a man beating the air. No, I beat my body to make it my slave so that after I have preached to others, I myself will not be disqualified for the prize" (1 Corinthians 9:26–27).

Here Paul was expressing a genuine fear, a real possibility. He had not yet completed the course. Even his vast experience and great successes did not make him immune to the subtle temptations of the body. In order that his ministry should not be short-circuited, he was willing to bring his bodily appetites under self-discipline as strict as that of the Spartan athletes in the arena.

The Christian leader is open to the danger of being defeated through overindulgence of physical appetites or through laziness. Such an acute danger calls for stern self-discipline. At the other end of the scale is an excess of physical activity, which can lead to fatigue and exhaustion. Leaders must be prepared to work even harder than their colleagues. But an exhausted person easily falls prey to the adversary. We should be alert to guard against both of these dangers.

He waged war with his thoughts. "The weapons we fight with are not the weapons of the world. On the contrary, they have divine power to demolish strongholds. We demolish arguments and every pretension that sets itself up against the knowledge of God, and we take captive every thought to make it obedient to Christ" (2 Corinthians 10:4–5). *(PL)*

Spiritual Wisdom

When men were to be selected for a subordinate leadership position within the church, one of the two prerequisite qualities specified was *wisdom*—an essential element for good leadership. "Brothers, choose seven men from among you who are known to be full of the Spirit and wisdom" (Acts 6:3).

True wisdom is more than knowledge, which is the basic accumulation of facts. It is more than mere intellectual ability. It is heavenly insight. Spiritual wisdom involves the knowledge of God and the intricacies of the human heart. It involves the right application of knowledge in moral and spiritual matters and in handling perplexing situations and complex human relationships. Wisdom is a quality that restrains leaders from rash or eccentric action, imparting a necessary balance in their approach.

The high place Paul gave to spiritual wisdom is seen in the way he constantly contrasted it with the ostentatious wisdom of the world. "Do not deceive yourselves. If any one of you thinks he is wise by the standards of this age, he should become a 'fool' so that he may become wise.

For the wisdom of this world is foolishness in God's sight" (1 Corinthians 3:18–19).

The need for wisdom was a frequent petition Paul raised in prayer for his converts and churches. "We have not stopped praying for you and asking God to fill you with the knowledge of his will through all spiritual wisdom and understanding" (Colossians 1:9).

Wisdom characterized the intentional method of Paul's preaching. "We proclaim [Christ], admonishing and teaching everyone with all wisdom, so that we may present everyone perfect in Christ" (Colossians 1:28). Wisdom inevitably characterizes the ministry of the Spirit-filled leader. "Let the word of Christ dwell in you richly as you teach and admonish one another with all wisdom" (Colossians 3:16).

To Paul we owe the revelation that "Christ Jesus . . . has become for us wisdom from God" (1 Corinthians 1:30). *(PL)*

The Lordship of Christ

The lordship of Christ was a constant emphasis of the apostle Paul. As he used the term in his writings, the title *Lord* uniformly denoted Christ. In his initial surrender, Paul embraced without reservation Christ's lordship and absolute mastery over his life. This totality of commitment was implicit in his question, "What shall I do, Lord?" (Acts 22:10). With quick spiritual insight, he realized that the purpose of Christ's death and resurrection went far beyond the mere salvation of the believer from judgment, but confirmed the authenticity of his lordship.

Paul later expressed the importance of Christ's lordship in these words: "For this very reason, Christ died and returned to life to that he might be the Lord of both the dead and the living" (Romans 14:9). It was the apostle's constant joy to emphasize "the crown rights of the Redeemer."

The greatest christological passage in the New Testament comes from Paul's pen in Philippians 2:5–11. In this poetic confession of faith, he first affirms the humiliation of the Son of God, calling attention to the Son's preexistence, incarnation, and crucifixion. Paul then unfolds the exaltation of the Son of Man, who shall be honored and worshiped eventually by all creation. In view of these glorious truths, the apostle exhorts, "Let this mind be in you, which was also in Christ Jesus" (Philippians 2:5 KJV).

"In Christ" is a particular phrase that appears quite often in many contexts in Paul's writings, a phrase that is especially pregnant with meaning. The idea behind the phrase seems to be that just as the sea is the sphere or element in which fish live, so Christians live in the sphere or element of Christ, joined to Him by an invisible yet inseparable bond. Every spiritual blessing is ours because we are *in Christ*—in a living, vital union with Him (Ephesians 1:3). *(PL)*

The Question of Church Discipline

One of the unwelcome responsibilities of the Christian leader is that of exercising a godly discipline. If scriptural standards and a wholesome moral and spiritual tone are to be maintained in a church or other Christian organization, it is sometimes necessary to exercise a loving and restorative discipline. This is especially the case when doctrinal error or moral failure is involved. Throughout his letters, Paul both encouraged and exemplified the exercise of such discipline.

It is noteworthy that he placed special emphasis on the spirit in which the disciplining is carried out. Harsh and unloving treatment simply alienates the offender, and that is not the purpose in view. "If anyone does not obey our instruction in this letter," Paul wrote, "take special note of him. Do not associate with him, in order that he may feel ashamed. Yet do not regard him as an enemy, but warn him as a brother" (2 Thessalonians 3:14–15).

In the case of the one who had "caused grief," the Corinthians were exhorted to "forgive and comfort him, so that he will not be overwhelmed by excessive sorrow.

I urge you, therefore, to reaffirm your love for him" (2 Corinthians 2:5, 7–8).

Both Scripture and experience agree that in any disciplinary action the following factors should be given full weight:

- Action should be taken only after a very thorough and impartial examination of all the facts has been made. The legal maxim, "Never accept a one-sided statement" would apply here.
- Genuine love should be the motivation of discipline, and any action should be conducted in the most considerate manner possible.
- Discipline should be undertaken only when it is clearly for the overall good of the individual and of the work of ministry.
- Discipline should be exercised only with much prayer.
- The paramount objective of discipline should be the spiritual help and restoration of the person concerned. *(PL)*

Remaining in Front

A leader must initiate. Some leaders are more gifted at conserving gains than starting new ventures, more gifted at maintaining order than generating ardor. True leaders must be adventurous as well as visionary. They must be ready to jump-start as well as hold speed. Paul constantly took calculated risks, always carefully and with much prayer, but always reaching for what lay beyond.

Leaders must either initiate plans for progress or recognize the worthy plans of others. They must remain in front, giving guidance and direction to those behind. They do not wait for things to happen, but rather make them happen. They are self-starters, always on the lookout for improved methods, eager to test new ideas.

Robert Louis Stevenson called the attitude of safety and security "that dismal fungus." Hudson Taylor took steps of faith that some people thought were wildcat schemes. The greatest achievements in the history of missions have come from leaders close to God who took courageous, calculated risks.

More failure comes from an excess of caution than from bold experiments with new ideas. A friend who filled an important global post in Christian outreach recently remarked that when he surveyed his life, most of his failures came from insufficient daring. The wife of Archbishop Mowell said, "The frontiers of the kingdom of God were never advanced by men and women of caution."

A leader cannot afford to ignore the counsel of cautious people who can give advice and help save a mission from mistakes and failure. But caution should not curb vision and initiative, especially when the leader knows God is in control.

To take responsibility willingly is the mark of a leader. Joshua was such a person. He did not hesitate to follow one of the greatest leaders of all history, Moses. Joshua had more reason than Moses to plead inadequacy, but Joshua did not repeat Moses' sin. Instead, he promptly accepted the task he was given and began the work.

When Elijah was taken up, Elisha did not flinch at stepping in. He accepted the authority conferred by the mantle of Elijah and became a leader in his own right.

In each case these leaders were assured of their divine calling. Once that issue is settled, no one should hesitate to answer God's call. *(PP)*

Interceding for Missionaries

EPHESIANS 6:18

How should we go about the work of intercession for missions so as to make the maximum contribution? Some suggestions for those who desire to become effective intercessors:

1. First and foremost, make a firm resolve and a deliberate decision, not without first counting the cost, to set aside time for regular intercession. Let only the most urgent interruptions break into this routine.

2. Ask the Lord to guide you to a special field of interest. Gather all the information you can and take an intelligent interest in a few missionaries and missionary situations. Endeavor to become literate in missionary matters.

3. Seek a personal link with some missionary for whom you can exercise a special prayer ministry as a prayer companion. Correspond with him or her and follow details of the work in prayer. Experience will enlarge your interests and guide your intercessions.

4. Have a prayer list on which you note the names of missionaries, perhaps praying for different continents on different days of the week.
5. Obtain literature on the places for which you desire to pray so that you have an intelligent grasp of strategic points on which to focus prayer. Learn what you can about the national people, leaders, and churches.
6. Do not become discouraged if results in the work for which you are praying seem meager. Is that really a reason for praying more earnestly?
7. Leave yourself open to God for Him to lay special prayer burdens on your heart. Such prayers can be mightily answered. *(PP)*

Inward Renewal

Therefore we do not lose heart, but though our outer man is decaying, yet our inner man is being renewed day by day. For light momentary affliction is producing for us an eternal weight of glory far beyond all comparison, while we look not at the things which are seen, but at the things which are not seen; for the things which are seen are temporal, but the things which are not seen are eternal (2 Corinthians 4:16–18 NASB).

The paragraph in which this text occurs balances six pairs of words: *outer* and *inner, decaying* and *renewed, light* and *weight, affliction* and *glory, seen* and *not seen, temporal* and *eternal.* Here is one of Paul's great secrets—the prescription for weakness is suffering. He well knew the peril of a spiritual wound on the battlefield, so he shares his own experience of God's upholding power with the Corinthian believers.

Actually the expression "we do not lose heart" is derived from military life and could be rendered "we do not act as deserters and cowards." We do not walk away from positions of trust even if they are dangerous, because we look to the glory ahead.

It is true that the outer man, which belongs to this temporal world, is decaying and suffers wear and tear. With advancing years, physical vigor wanes and beauty fades. Old age and death advance with a relentless step, and those whose lives are governed only by sight and time are weighed down and depleted. But "we do not lose heart," as Paul states.

Here is the blessed paradox: our outer man is *decaying,* our inner man is *renewed.* The inner man is rejuvenated in the "divine beauty parlor" by the Holy Spirit. Each new day brings a fresh provision of divine strength. What a cheering revelation from Paul! By a divine alchemy, God harnesses the very forces that destroy the outer person to develop the inner person. And this renewal goes on day by day. There are no idle days with the Holy Spirit!

This was the reason Paul was able to view with a larger perspective the wasting away of his outer man through persecution, disease, and innumerable hardships. It enabled him to make the incredible statement, "[I] glory in tribulations" (Romans 5:3 KJV), because he knew that the Holy Spirit used these experiences to mature him and to strengthen his inner man. *(CC)*

Nehemiah's Leadership Objectives

*N*ehemiah recovered the authority of the Word of God in the lives of the people (8:1–8). The reforms he instituted would have been short-lived or even impossible apart from that. He restored the Feast of Tabernacles, which had not been observed since Joshua's day. He led the people to repentance through the reading of the Law (9:3–5). He purified the temple of pagan influence (13:4–9). He encouraged tithing, established the Sabbath rest, forbade intermarriage with pagan foreigners, and thus here covered the special identity of Israel as God's chosen people.

Nehemiah could organize projects and people well. Before making detailed plans, he conducted a careful survey of the situation (2:11–16). He made a detailed assessment of the personnel available. He did not neglect tedious paperwork. He then established key objectives, assigned those to responsible leaders (men of faith and piety), and set them to work (7:1–3). He gave adequate recognition to subordinate leaders, mentioning them by name and the place where each worked (3:1–32). They were given a sense that they were more than mere cogs in a machine. He practiced a wise delegation of responsibility. He stated, "I put in charge of Jerusalem my brother Hanani, along with Hananiah the commander of the citadel" (7:2). He had high standards for the subordinates whom he chose, selecting Hananiah, for example, "because he was a man of integrity and feared God more than most men do" (7:2). All of this opened the leadership potential of others.

Nehemiah faced up to opposition without forcing a violent confrontation. He accepted insults, innuendo, and treachery. He walked through it with his head high and his eyes wide open, with much prayer (4:9). When he could, he simply ignored his adversaries. He always took precautions (v. 16). He never allowed opposition to deflect his energy from the central task. He always kept faith in God (v. 20).

The test of spiritual leadership is the achievement of its objective. In Nehemiah's case, the record is clear: "So the wall was completed" (6:15). *(SL)*

The Slowness of God

In time of war, bleeding hearts cry, "God could bring all this slaughter and bloodshed to an end in a moment. Why does He wait? Why does He not intervene?"

Why not? It is certainly not because He is physically unable or that He is unwilling to do so. The only answer is that He is *morally* unable to do so. We must recognize that there are things that are moral and spiritual impossibilities to God. He cannot lie. He cannot deny Himself. He cannot save a sinful person apart from repentance and faith. God does not glory in war and bloodshed, and He will intervene when it is morally right to do so. When He sees a nation bow in humiliation and confession of its national sins, it becomes possible and right for Him to intervene. When wicked Nineveh publicly expressed its repentance, God immediately responded by lifting the judgment. It is not God who is too slow, but people who are too sinful.

How slow God sometimes seems in granting the answer to our prayers! Months and even years go by and yet there is no apparent response. George Muller prayed for more than sixty years for the salvation of two men. The answer came in the case of one of the men just before Muller's death and the other one shortly after. What a long, drawn-out test of faith this was, but how wonderful the prayer of faith proved to be to the one who prayed.

Sometimes God is slow in granting the answer to our prayers so that we may learn lessons we could master in no other way. We pray for the salvation or the sanctification of our children, and the answer sometimes seems more remote than ever. But God has not forgotten His promises. It is for us to maintain the attitude of confident faith as exemplified by Abraham, who relied on the Word of God.

"With undaunted faith he looked at the facts . . . he refused to allow any distrust of a definite pronouncement of God to make him waver. He drew strength from his faith, and . . . remained absolutely convinced that God was able to implement his own promise" (Romans 4:19–21 PHILLIPS). *(SP)*

The Greatest Is Love

Let us speak the truth by all means, but let it be in love.

The power to unravel "all mysteries," the possessions of profound erudition, the ability to plumb and propound the deep things of God—all these count for nothing in the absence of love. As Matthew Henry put it, "A clear and deep head is of no significance without a benevolent and loving heart." Love is more than knowledge.

Love triumphs over miracle-working faith. No believer should minimize the value and importance of faith in every aspect of the Christian life, and Paul certainly did not. The vital part it plays cannot be overestimated, for "without faith it is impossible to please God" (Hebrews 11:6). But it should always be remembered that "faith worketh by love" (Galatians 5:6 KJV). If faith is out of proportion to love, her apparent success is really failure. Even the receiving of spectacular answers to prayer is no acceptable substitute for a love-filled life. We have often prayed, "Lord, increase our faith," but someone has suggested the addition of another petition: "Lord, increase our love, lest our faith be in vain." Love is more than faith.

The superlative excellence of faith over heartless charity is emphasized. Few activities secure our approval more than philanthropy, and rightly so. Yet, "if I share out all my goods morsel by morsel, but have not love, it profiteth me nothing," says Deissman. The purity of the motive determines the quality of the action. Ananias emulated Barnabas in making a magnificent gift, but his unworthy motive robbed the act of all spiritual value and rendered the gift wholly unacceptable to God. We should closely scrutinize the motive that prompts our philanthropy lest love of attention or desire for approval displace true love of others. Love is more than philanthropy. *(SP)*

The Need to Evangelize

It is to be kept in mind that the generations do not wait for the convenience of the Church in respect to their evangelization. Men are born and die, whether or not Christians are ready to give them the gospel. And so if the Church of any generation does not evangelize the heathen of that generation, those heathen will never be evangelized at all . . . It is always true in the work of evangelization that the present can never anticipate the future, and that the future can never replace the past. What is to be done in soul-saving for any generation must be done by that generation. —Dr. H. W. Frost.

If we argue that there must be a way of entrance into the kingdom of heaven other than the way of faith in Christ for those who have never heard, then we cut away the central core of our purpose and are left only with the certainty of material philanthropy toward those we wish to serve. The idea removes all urgency from our task. We know the reality of hell, and we know the way to escape. How shall we escape if we neglect to warn and woo the unevangelized?

A student once asked C. H. Spurgeon if he thought the heathen who had never heard the gospel would be saved. The great preacher answered, "It is more a question with me whether we who have the gospel and fail to give it to those who have not, can be saved."

The words of Ion Keith Falconer of Arabia, though spoken to a past generation, have continued relevance for the new generation of young people today: "While vast continents lie shrouded in midnight darkness, and hundreds of millions still suffer the horrors of heathendom and Islam, the burden of proof rests on you to show the circumstances in which God has placed you were meant to keep you out of the mission field." *(HL)*

Love Is Patient and Kind

"Love suffereth long." It is significant that the patience of love comes first. It is not so much what love can do as how long love can be sustained without breaking down, for it is our long-suffering with others that is addressed in this passage. Love's severest tests come in the realm of our relations with others. "Lord, how oft shall my brother sin against me and I forgive him? till seven times?" Peter doubtless thought he was being very generous until he heard the Master's reply: "I say not unto thee, Until seven times: but, Until seventy times seven" (Matthew 18:21–22 KJV).

Love does not balk at the first hurdle but finishes the race. No matter how strong the provocation, love is never betrayed by ill-advised speech or hasty action that will later be bitterly regretted. Love knows how to hold its peace even amid gross injustice. Love's long-suffering found its crowning demonstration on the slopes of Mount Calvary, where the supreme sufferer, instead of calling down curses, prayed for His tormentors.

"Love is kind." Kindness has been defined as a way to place oneself at the disposal of others, regardless of their position or attitude. What a benediction kind people are in a cold and unsympathetic world. They are always on the lookout to be of service to someone else.

Lady Bartle Frere once requested a young guest to meet her husband at the railway station.

"But how shall I recognize him?" asked the young man. "I have never met him."

"Just look for a tall gentleman helping someone" was the response. "That will be my husband." *(SP)*

Dealing with Jealousy

NUMBERS 12:3

*M*ost leaders at some time face the problem of a jealous rival. Even Moses encountered that test. Jealousy is a common weapon of the devil.

Moses' first such challenge came from within his own family—his sister and brother. They had apparently forgotten that without Moses' self-sacrificing response to the divine call to lead the people out of Egypt, they and all the rest of Israel would still be living under the slave master's lash.

Miriam by this time was an elderly woman, and her experience of God should have taught her the evil and ugliness of jealousy. She prompted gossip against Moses because of his marriage to an Ethiopian. Race hatred is not the sin of recent centuries alone. Miriam resented the intrusion of a foreigner and drew the weakling Aaron into her rebellion.

Not content with second place, Miriam and Aaron, led by the devil, tried to remove Moses by a coup. They cloaked their treachery in piety: "Has the Lord spoken only through Moses? Hasn't he also spoken through us?"

Moses was deeply wounded, but he said nothing to vindicate himself. His main concern was God's glory, not his own position or privilege. "Now Moses was a very humble man, more humble than anyone else on the face of the earth" (Numbers 12:3). Yet though Moses maintained a dignified silence, God would not allow such a challenge to the authority of His servant to go without response.

Because the offense was public, judgment and punishment would also be public. "When the cloud lifted from above the Tent, there stood Miriam—leprous, like snow," the record runs (12:10). Such a drastic punishment points to the gravity of her sin, and once again Moses' greatness shines. His only response was to pray for his sister, and God graciously responded in mercy.

The lesson for the leader is plain. The person who fills a role appointed by God need not worry about vindicating his or her work when rivals become jealous or treacherous. Such a leader is safe in the hands of a heavenly Protector. *(SL)*

No Double Standard

Some time ago a contributor to a missionary fund sent a check for twenty-five pounds. In the covering letter he stated that his family desired a new radio, but he was unwilling to spend so much on a luxury when there was such urgent need on the mission field. Finally he resolved the problem by deciding that for every luxury they bought for themselves, he would devote an equivalent amount to Christian work—an example worthy of emulation.

It cannot be too strongly stated that the New Testament does not promote two standards of living—one for the Christian worker or missionary whose support comes from the Lord's treasury and another for the businessperson or worker at home. The missionary is equally entitled to the luxuries we enjoy at home if it comes to the matter of rights. If we have a car in the interests of our work, why shouldn't the missionary have a car for his or her work? Since all we have is a gift and trust from our sovereign Lord, why should there be a double standard? Among followers of a cross-bearing Christ, the sacrifices in the interests of the gospel should be similar, with only a difference in circumstances. In time of war we recognize that we all sacrifice to the extent that we are able.

Is this principle less applicable in the ceaseless spiritual warfare in which we are engaged?

One final method adopted by Satan was titled by the late Dr. A. J. Gordon "extra-corpus benevolence." The deceiver persuades victims to postpone their generosity until after death by bequeathing a substantial sum to Christian organizations. Dr. Gordon emphasized the fact that a reward was promised in Scriptures only for deeds done in the body. Christians are, of course, justified in making adequate provision for their dependents, but can it be truly called giving to God when, having made provision for their responsibilities, they hold onto the surplus until death shakes it from their pockets?

Great blessing has come to many who have put their money to work for the Lord during their lifetime. This is a true storing of treasure in heaven. After speaking on this theme on one occasion, I was summoned by a businessman who said that he was that day disbursing nine thousand pounds that he had left to various missionary societies in his will. He thus had the joy of seeing the fruit of his gift in this lifetime. *(SP)*

Loyalty to the Master

hy did our Lord make His terms of discipleship so exacting, when the inevitable result would be the loss of popular support? It was because He was concerned more with quality than with quantity. He desired a band of chosen men and women, a Gideon's band, on whose unwavering devotion He could count in days of crisis. He wanted trustworthy disciples on whom He could rely when building His church or battling with the powers of evil (Luke 14:29, 31). Once disciples are convinced of the majesty and the glory of the Christ they follow and of the cause in which they are enlisted, they will be willing for any sacrifice.

Several centuries ago an invading Eastern king, whose march had met with unbroken success, neared the territory of the young chieftain Abu Taber. Hearing of his valor, the king was reluctant to kill him and instead sent an ambassador with terms of peace. When he heard the proposal, Abu Taber summoned one of his soldiers, handed him a dagger, and commanded, "Plunge this into your breast." The soldier obeyed and fell dead at his feet. Calling another, he ordered, "Leap over that precipice into the Euphrates." Without a moment's hesitation he leaped to his death. Turning to the ambassador Abu said, "Go, tell your master I have five hundred men like that, and within twenty-four hours I will have him chained with my dogs." The king with his greatly superior numbers continued his advance, but numbers were of no avail against the fierce loyalty of Abu Taber's devotees. Before a day had passed, the king was chained with Abu's dogs. It is the quality of loyalty that is important.

Christianity truly interpreted has never been popular. Indeed, a religion that is popular is far removed from the teaching of our Lord. "Woe unto you, when all men shall speak well of you! for so did their fathers to the false prophets," He warned (Luke 6:26 KJV). On the contrary, Christians are truly blessed when people revile them and say all manner of evil against them falsely for Christ's sake (Matthew 5:11). We are invited to share not His popularity, but His unpopularity. *(SM)*

Cleansing by the Blood

The record of the Passover night in Exodus 12 represents the blood of the innocent victim applied in faith as availing to hold back the execution of judgment on the Israelites. Because of the blood, the avenger becomes the protector.

Another twofold picture is presented in Leviticus 16, which details the ritual of the great Day of Atonement. The death of Christ is there represented as both satisfying the righteous claims of God against the sinning person and forever bearing away his or her polluted sins "unto a land not inhabited" (v. 22 KJV).

In Numbers 19, read in conjunction with Hebrews 9:13–14, we are introduced to Christ's death as a continual provision for the constant cleansing of Christians as they walk amid the inescapable impurities of their daily life. It is God's provision for the maintenance of unbroken communion with Him. Sins of the future are in view as well as sins of the past and sins of which we are unconscious as well as those of which we are conscious.

There is no possibility of forsaking sin entirely. But we have the power over sin. This harmonizes entirely with Paul's question and answer, "Shall we continue in sin . . .

God forbid" (Romans 6:1–2). The objectives John had in view for the believers were clearly expressed: "My little children, these things write I unto you, that ye sin not" (1 John 2:1 KJV). But in the same passage, he recognizes the possibility of sinning and reveals the remedy for such a condition. Sinning is no longer necessary, but it is possible and therefore must be provided for. The lifeboat is provided, not because the vessel must sink, but in case it does. The work of Christ under consideration was such a divine provision. It is one of the richest in spiritual teaching of the Old Testament types and will amply repay close study, for Paul assures us that "all these things happened unto them for examples: and they are written for our admonition, upon whom the ends of the world are come" (1 Corinthians 10:11 KJV). *(SP)*

The Sacrifice of Christ

Like the chosen victim, Christ was without spot or blemish. Through the miracle of the virgin birth and the activity of the Holy Spirit, He escaped the taint of original sin. His purity was essential and inherent. No matter how severe the criticism to which He was subjected during His life on earth, it was demonstrated that "in him is no sin" (1 John 3:5). The yoke of sin never rested on His shoulders, nor was it under a yoke of constraint that He consented to become the sacrifice for our sins. His sacrifice was absolutely voluntary.

Then, too, like the victim, Christ, in order "that he might sanctify the people with his own blood, suffered without the gate" of Jerusalem (Hebrews 13:12 KJV), the defiled place frequented by the lepers. The defilement was viewed as transferred to the victim that must now take the place of the defiled person—outside the camp. In this act of matchless condescension on the part of the Lord of glory, the boundless and forgiving love of God is exhibited. The sprinkling of the blood before the tabernacle did not in itself affect the cleansing of the polluted person, but before there can be purification there must first be atonement.

The burning of the cedar and hyssop bound with scarlet wool signifies that the sinful self-life, the "old man," whether in attractive or repulsive guise, was cast into the burning or, to use the New Testament terminology, was crucified with Christ, and in Him was done away with (Romans 6:6 RSV). The self-life will always defile and pollute us unless we put it to death (Romans 6:11). We must resolutely disregard its plea to be allowed to come down from the cross.

The ashes, evidence of a completed sacrifice, were regarded as the concentration of the essential properties of the offering. They were incorruptible, and therefore a suitable emblem of the perfection and everlasting efficacy of the sacrifice of Christ. The ashes laid up in a clean place represent the store of merit there is in the Lord Jesus, perpetually preserved for the removal of the daily pollution of sin. The smallest quantity of the concentrated ash would suffice to cleanse. Jewish tradition records that only six heifers were required in all Jewish history. "If . . . the ashes of a heifer . . . how much more will the blood of Christ . . . cleanse" (Hebrews 9:13 NASB)? *(SP)*

The Indwelling of Christ

Christianity is the only religion in which the founder claims to live in the very beings of those who place their faith in Him. Neither Buddha nor Muhammad made any such claim. This is the unique characteristic of the Christian faith and what makes its benefits far superior to those of other religions.

Early in His ministry, our Lord spoke about His dwelling in His followers. "At that day ye shall know that I am in my Father, and ye in me, and I in you" (John 14:20 KJV). The lover of our souls will not be content with mere influence in our lives. He must dwell in our hearts, in very intimate fellowship with us. Paul included this concept as an article of his message—"Christ in you, the hope of glory" (Colossians 1:27 KJV). John rejoiced in its reality— "Greater is he that is in you, than he that is in the world" (1 John 4:4 KJV).

This personal indwelling of Christ is both a fact to comprehend and an experience to realize. There is a difference between a fact and an experience of that fact. Whether we are conscious of it or not, Christ indwells every Christian all the time. It may seem mysterious, but so are many other things about the universe we cannot understand. I am not conscious of the blood flowing in my veins, but that does not alter the fact that it does. Through failing to realize that Christ really indwells them, many believers never go on to fully appreciate and utilize this blessed fact.

Jesus had promised, "At that day ye shall know that I am . . . in you." To what day did He refer? The answer was given on the day of Pentecost when the Holy Spirit was given as Christ's representative on earth. With the gift of the Spirit, there came to the waiting disciples an overwhelming consciousness of the spiritual presence and indwelling of the physically absent Christ that transformed them into His fearless and selfless servants.

"When it pleased God . . . to reveal His Son in [Paul]," the experience was so real and vivid to the apostle that he testified, "I am crucified with Christ: nevertheless, I live; yet not I, but Christ liveth in me" (Galatians 2:20 KJV). Do you realize that Jesus Christ is in you? *(CC)*

The Satanic World System

What is the "world" spoken of in Scripture of which Satan is god? To differentiate this word—*kosmos*—from other words translated *world,* it might be helpful to adopt the term *world system,* for that is its connotation. The *world,* as Paul and John used it, is human society organized in such a way as to exclude God and to make Him superfluous. It refers to the great evil system over which Satan exercises dictatorial power. Its master principles are not love and self-sacrifice, but selfishness, greed, ambition, pleasure, and coercion (Matthew 4:8–9; John 12:31; 18:36; Ephesians 2:2; 1 John 2:15–17).

"We know," wrote John, "that the whole world lies in the power of the evil one" (1 John 5:19 NASB). As its presiding mastermind, Satan dictates its objectives and plots its policies. The world embraces all unregenerate people, whether attractive or unlovable, because they are united in a common desire and purpose to be independent of God. It is called "this evil world," and it hates the Christ who testified of it "that its deeds are evil" (John 7:7).

Concerning this satanic world system, C. I. Scofield writes: "It is imposing and powerful with armies and fleets; is often outwardly religious, scientific, cultured, and elegant; but seeching with national and commercial rivalries and ambitions; is upheld in any real crisis only by armed force, and is dominated by satanic principles."

It was the kingdoms of this world that the devil offered Jesus in the wilderness. The expression *the kingdoms of the world* used by Satan in the temptation was in common use to describe the Roman Empire, which grasped most of the known world in its tentacles. The control of the world was surrendered to Satan by the first man, who yielded his God-given sovereignty over the earth and creation to him. Even after Calvary's victory, when Christ won back our forfeited inheritance, Satan's control of this world system has been permitted to continue for reasons that God deems wise.

It is not difficult to recognize the hallmark of satanic control of the world system in the corruption, deceit, and pollution that characterizes its policies and politics. *(SN)*

Imitating Christ

"Be imitators of me, just as I also am of Christ" (1 Corinthians 11:1 NASB). Paul purposely modeled his life on that of his Master. His actions and attitudes were calculated to accurately reflect the character of his Lord. So effective and sincere was he, that he actually had the boldness to exhort the Corinthian Christians to copy him as he copied Christ. Who of us would dare to make a similar challenge? Yet the quality of Paul's life of unselfish service to others gave him the right to exhort them in this way. We too should live this way ourselves so that others may safely imitate us.

We should imitate Paul in his honest self-appraisal: "Who then is Paul . . . but [a servant] by whom ye believed?" (1 Corinthians 3:5 KJV). "Though I preach the gospel, I have nothing to glory of" (1 Corinthians 9:16 KJV). "[I] will not boast of things without [my] measure" (2 Corinthians 10:13 KJV). Paul knew his limitations and did not suffer from an inflated ego.

His strong support of others was another Christlike quality that we may well copy. He did not hesitate to delegate responsibility to younger colleagues and was lavish in his appreciation. "[I have sent] you Timotheus, who is my beloved son, and faithful in the Lord" (1 Corinthians 4:17 KJV). He delighted to associate Titus with himself on terms of equality—"Titus . . . my partner and fellow-helper" (2 Corinthians 8:23 KJV).

He demonstrated a sensitive respect for the rights of others. He was always considerate in his relations with others. "Without thy mind would I do nothing," were his words to Philemon (14 KJV). He showed a similar respect for the convictions of others. "Not that we lord it over your faith" (2 Corinthians 1:24). People of strong convictions are not always willing to concede equal liberty to the convictions of others.

His compassionate reaction to a lack of appreciation among the Corinthians should stir us to act likewise: "I will very gladly spend and be spent for you; though the more abundantly I love you, the less I be loved" (2 Corinthians 12:15 KJV). Certain aromatic leaves do not release their perfume until they are crushed! Paul's rejection demonstrates these qualities.

We should imitate him in his insatiable passion for advancing the gospel. He prayed for an enlarged sphere of influence so that he might "preach the gospel in the regions beyond you" (2 Corinthians 10:16 KJV). He was determined to reach the regions beyond his comfort level. Are we? *(CC)*

Acceptable Worship

No worship is acceptable to God that ignores or excludes Christ. It is through Christ alone that we have access to the Father. "By him we have access to the Father." "No man cometh unto the Father, but by me," claimed Jesus. To worship Christ is to worship God, who has revealed Himself in Christ. "He that hath seen me hath seen the Father."

How can we really come to know the Christ who alone reveals God? The answer is, of course, in the Bible, the only tangible means of divine knowledge. "Search the scriptures," said Jesus, "they are they which testify of me" (John 5:39 KJV). In them is the complete and satisfying revelation and interpretation of Jesus Christ. Failure both in worship and in other aspects of prayer is directly traceable to our misuse or ignorance of the Word of God.

The Scriptures are rich in material to stimulate and feed worship. Vast tracts of truth await our exploration and exploitation. God's sovereignty, holiness, love, mercy, patience, faithfulness, wisdom, and grace are evidenced in every book. It is for us to make intelligent use of this divinely inspired prayer book. It is essential that we have

71

a true conception of Christ, lest we be found worshiping a god of our own imagining.

Let it not be thought that worship consists primarily in pleasing emotions and lofty thoughts. It is inseparably united with service. Those who worship their God most devoutly will serve Him most sacrificially. Note the conjunction of the two ideas: "Thou shalt *worship* the Lord thy God, and him only shalt thou *serve* (Matthew 4:10 KJV, emphasis added)." We must not disconnect what God has joined. Worship is no substitute for service, and service is no substitute for worship. True worship on Sunday will express itself in sacrificial service on Monday. To worship is to serve. The blessedness of worship will not stop at service; it will produce transformed character. Inevitably we become increasingly like the blessed One whom we worship. *(SP)*

Comfort to Comfort Others

lessed be the God and Father of our Lord Jesus Christ, the Father of mercies and God of all comfort, who comforts us in all our affliction so that we will be able to comfort those who are in any affliction with the comfort with which we ourselves are comforted by God" (2 Corinthians 1:3–4). One of the great preachers of the twentieth century, sensitive to the needs of his generation, declared that if he could live his life over again, he would devote more time to the ministry of comfort and encouragement. His assessment of a preacher's role still applies today.

Isaiah described the mission of the Messiah as ministering to the poor, the brokenhearted, the captives, and the blind. God is deeply concerned for His burdened and suffering children. As the "God of all comfort," He comforts them in their sorrows, but with a definite end in view: that their experience of His comfort might equip them to comfort others. Are we using God's comfort ultimately to benefit others, or do we selfishly keep it to ourselves?

The English word *comfort,* used ten times in five verses, is an inadequate translation of the word in Greek. This comfort is more than soothing sympathy; it is comfort that brings strength and courage, a courage that enables us to meet and triumph over the worst that life can bring to us. Interestingly, the word has a derivation similar to *Paraclete,* one of the names of the Holy Spirit, who imparts God's comfort to us.

The personal experience of God's comfort qualifies us to comfort others. If we ourselves experience little trouble and affliction, we won't have a valid ministry of comfort and encouragement to others. God's comfort was one of the main sources of grace that enabled Paul to make the astounding claim that he rejoiced in tribulation. It is one of the consolations of gray hair that, having experienced God's comfort in our times of sorrow and trials of all kinds, we are able to use our experience to bring similar comfort to others. Are we really treating our experience as an investment in the lives of others? If we do, our own burdens will be lightened by sharing how God has comforted us in the past.

"It is possible to escape a multitude of troubles," said J. H. Jowett, "by living an insignificant life. The range of our possible suffering is determined by the largeness and nobility of our aims." Let us covet this ministry of comfort and encouragement. *(CC)*

Weakness and Strength

"God hath chosen the weak things of the world to confound the things which are mighty" (1 Corinthians 1:27 KJV). This is very disillusioning to the complacent and self-sufficient Christian but tremendously encouraging to those who feel weak and inadequate. The latter tend to shrink from attempting any difficult task for God and use their own insufficiency as an excuse. We maintain that we are too weak. Yet God says that is the very reason He chose us and put us in the front rank of His conquering army. "God hath chosen the weak things . . . to confound the . . . mighty" (1 Corinthians 1:27).

An important spiritual principle is involved, which must be grasped if we are to realize the full spiritual possibilities of our lives. God can achieve His purposes either through the absence of human power and resources or the abandonment of reliance on them. All through history God has chosen and used "nobodies" in the eyes of the world, because their very weakness created such an unusual dependence on Him, making possible the unique display of His power. He chose and used the "somebodies" only when they renounced dependence on their natural abilities and resources.

75

Paul does not say that God did the best He could with such poor material but that He purposely selected them and overlooked others, passing over the wise and the mighty. It is a revolutionary concept that God will not use me in spite of my weakness but actually because of it. Human weakness provides the best backdrop for the exercise of divine strength. "My strength is made perfect in weakness" (2 Corinthians 12:9 KJV) is God's word. "When I am weak, then am I strong" is Paul's testimony (2 Corinthians 12:10 KJV). "Out of weakness [they] were made strong" (Hebrews 11:34 KJV) was the experience of the heroes of faith.

Here is something to encourage and lift us in time of discouragement or depression. It is good to realize our weakness and say, "Who is sufficient for these things?" (2 Corinthians 2:16 KJV). But we should remember that this is matched with "Our sufficiency is of God" (2 Corinthians 3:5 KJV). *(CC)*

God Behind the Scenes

One notable feature of the book of Esther is the absence of any mention of the name of God. But although His name is not pronounced, it is latent; and His hidden activity is everywhere to be seen by the discerning eye. In a theater, the scene-shifter is not seen, but the whole audience enjoys the benefits of that hidden activity. God does not always work ostentatiously, but He is nonetheless active, and the outcome of events will demonstrate His providential control.

Follow the timeline in the story. It seemed as though God had delayed His intervention too long, for Mordecai was to be hanged the very next morning, and no possible plan for his deliverance was apparent. Who could intervene on his behalf? But while God may not be early, He is never late. At the last possible moment, He intervened in a most natural way. When the hour struck on God's clock, the righteous man was delivered and the wicked man punished. The whole reversal of events occurred overnight and was orchestrated through a king's insomnia.

What outcome could be more fitting than the exact reversal of the positions of the wicked Haman and the virtuous Mordecai? The honor that the former planned for himself was enjoyed by the latter, while the gallows erected for the latter were occupied by the former. Where, as seems so often the case, just retribution does not fall on the wrongdoer during this life, the certainty of final and just judgment must take place.

Whether in individual or in national affairs, all is foreseen, foreordained, and permitted. Everything proceeds under God's direction. *God's perfect plan will become plain if we have the patience to wait.* Mordecai was doubtless mystified by the apparent inactivity of God; but after his patience had been tested to the limit, it was rewarded. So even though we may not see God's fully matured plan in this life, we shall wonder as we see it unfold in the hereafter and be awed by its perfection. *(SP)*

The Inner Circle

Were Peter, James, and John specially selected by the Lord? With Him there is no caprice or favoritism. After He chose them, their relationship with Him was the result of their own choice. It is a sobering thought that we too are as close to Christ as we intentionally choose to be. The deepening intimacy of these three with Jesus resulted from the depth of their response to His love and training.

They recognized that intimacy with Him involved responsibility as well as conferred privilege. The Master had told them, "Whoever does God's will is my brother and sister and mother" (Mark 3:35). Some ties are closer even than those of blood relationship.

What excluded some disciples from the inner circle? If *perfection* were the criterion, then Peter the denier and James and John, who wanted special recognition, would have been excluded. But they were included. If it were *temperament*, then surely the volatile Peter, and James and John, the fire-eaters of Samaria, would not have gained entrance.

Why then did John have the primacy in the group? He alone grasped the place of privilege that was available to all. It was *love* that drew John into a deeper intimacy with

Jesus than the other apostles. Jesus loved them all, but John alone claimed the title "the disciple whom Jesus loved." If Jesus loved John more, it was because John loved Him more. Mutual love and confidence are the keys to intimacy.

It would seem that admittance to the inner circle of deepening intimacy with God is the outcome of *deep desire*. Only those who count such intimacy a prize worth sacrificing anything else for are likely to attain it. If other intimacies are more desirable to us, we will not gain entry to that circle.

The place on Jesus' breast is still vacant and open to any who are willing to pay the price of deepening intimacy. We are now, and we will be in the future, only as intimate with God as we intentionally choose to be. *(EI)*

The Joy of Friendship

JOHN 15:15

he man after God's heart will reflect the attitude of the One who chose to call frail men His friends. No longer do I call you slaves; . . . I have called you friends" (John 15:15 NASB). David's capacity for friendship was one of the qualities that made him a man after God's heart.

Friendship fosters intimacy, and in times of difficulty and danger it is a great strength to have a staunch friend alongside. God gave David that compensation in Jonathan, Saul's son. In their association, these men have given us an example of ideal friendship.

David befriended unfortunate men who had no friends and won from them an almost fanatical love and loyalty. His followers in the cave of Adullam were a motley group of outlaws, outcasts, and misfits. Yet from that unpromising material, he molded an elite and powerful fighting force. Like Jesus, David was the friend of publicans and sinners.

He was a natural leader, possessing charm and charisma that won the love and loyalty of his men. He had only to breathe a wish for a drink from the familiar well at Bethlehem for his men to risk their lives to obtain it for him. Not only was he a natural leader, but also he was a loyal, considerate friend to those who threw in their lot with him.

Jonathan's self-effacing friendship with him stands out in sharp relief against the jealousy and betrayal of his father, Saul. It is one of the mysteries of life that such a father should have such a son, in whom malice and self-seeking were displaced by magnanimity and integrity.

David and Jonathan were soul mates—men of similar tastes and interests—and they displayed the same spirit in times of testing. Jonathan's renunciation of his throne in favor of his friend and rival is one of the noblest acts of history. There are some friendships that weaken, but Jonathan "strengthened [David's] hand in God." The one who is privileged to enjoy the intimacy of such a friendship is indeed fortunate. *(EI)*

The World Hates the Church

Christian should not expect sympathy and consideration from a hostile, satanically controlled society. Because believers are identified with Christ, they should expect to share some of the hostility He experienced.

The world loves its own people who adopt its standards and share its interests, but it hates those who will not conform (John 15:19). The early Christians who remained loyal to the faith were denounced as cannibals, immoral people, and disloyal revolutionaries. Only in compromising one's position can a Christian maintain friendly relations with the world. Intimacy with Christ inevitably draws the hatred of the world, as His disciples discovered.

Logically, the enemy of the Master will be the enemy of His servant. The servant need not expect more considerate treatment than his Master. The comforting factor is that our Master shares our rejection by the world and appreciates the fact that it is because of our loyalty to Him. Nor will our loyalty lack its reward.

In a few sharp words, Jesus diagnosed the cause of the world's hatred. If He had not come, they could have gone along comfortably in their sin, but "Now . . . they have no excuse for their sin." He had laid bare their hypocrisy and deceit and exposed their evil designs. Now they hated Him and included His followers in their hostility.

How were the disciples to meet and overcome that hatred? It was through the ministry of the Holy Spirit. "When the Helper comes, whom I will send to you from the Father . . . He will testify about Me, and you will testify also" (15:26–27 NASB). Jesus did not remove His disciples from this hostile world but empowered them for witness to it through the power of the Spirit (Acts 1:8). That power is equally available for those disciples who are the objects of the world's hostility in this day. *(EI)*

The Law of Love

Christ sets His own love before us as a model. "A new commandment I give to you, that you love one another, even as I have loved you, that you also love one another" (John 13:34 NASB). The law of love goes further than loving one's neighbors as oneself; it is to love one another as we love Him. It is love that takes no thought of the cost. That was the active principle of Christ's life. Paul, too, exhorts us to "live a life of love, just as Christ loved us and gave himself up for us as a fragrant offering and sacrifice to God" (Ephesians 5:2).

Personal preferences or dislikes have nothing to do with love. We are to love people whom we do not even like. "If you love those who love you, what credit is that to you? Even sinners love those who love them" (Luke 6:32). Although there may be those I do not like, I can still will to love them. It is the will and not the emotions that is supreme.

"He who has My commandments and keeps them is the one who loves Me; and he who loves Me will be loved by My Father, and I will love him and will disclose Myself to him" (John 14:21 NASB). Obedience is the test of love, and it is rewarded by deepening intimacy. Nothing is said here about emotional reactions—only simple obedience. The key question is not, "How do you feel?" but, "Have you obeyed?" Love is expressed through the will. If we are living obediently, we have John 14:21 as our assurance that we love Him and He loves us. One timid Christian said, "I think I love Him because there are things I refrain from doing for no other reason than that He forbids them, while I do other things simply because He desires them." He passes the test. If Christ's will is to us the law of our lives, His smile of approval will be an adequate reward. *(EI)*

Intimacy through Growing Love

In His memorable private discussion with Peter after his denial, the Lord made it clear to His penitent friend that the future would require of Peter an unwavering devotion to Himself. Three times He probed Peter's conscience to its depths with the searching query, "Simon, son of John, do you love me?" (John 21:15–17). He knew that if Peter gave Him his unqualified love and devotion, he could then be entrusted as a spiritual shepherd, with the sensitive task of strengthening his brethren. Increasing intimacy would develop only through growing love.

Paul's experience of intimacy with Christ only fed the flames of a passion to know Him still better: "That I may know Him and the power of His resurrection and the fellowship of His sufferings, being conformed to His death" (Philippians 3:10 NASB).

Paul had been assuring the believers at Philippi that his deepest concern was not his ancestry, achievements, or prestige, but the attaining of a deeper fellowship with his Lord. "But whatever things were gain to me, those things I have counted as loss for the sake of Christ. More than that, I count all things to be loss in view of the surpassing value of knowing Christ Jesus my Lord, for whom I have suffered the loss of all things, and count them but rubbish so that I may gain Christ" (Philippians 3:7–8 NASB). For such an inestimable reward, no price was too great.

All spiritual ministry flows from the reality of our knowledge of God and the vitality of our fellowship with Him and His Son. A successful, fruitful ministry does not just happen—it is purchased by surrender of all we possess. The more influential the ministry is, the steeper the price will be. It cannot be paid in a lump sum; we pay for it in gradually increasing installments as the challenges increase. There is no such thing as a cheap, fruitful ministry. *(EI)*

Simple Obedience

It is well to remember that a great many matters that call for our decision are already taken care of. The sphere in which we have to decide is not so large as we may think, but it does include some very crucial issues.

Consider these areas in which it is not prayer for guidance that is required, but simple obedience:

Clear, unequivocal statements of scriptural principle. The Bible gives general guidance on all matters of morals, ethics, spiritual life, family life, and church life. The question we have to answer is, "What does the Bible have to say in principle or by example on this subject?"

Claims of duty. Relationships impose duties. We have fundamental duties in the areas of family, business, profession, church, and community. There will be minor decisions to make within the scope of particular fundamental duties. For example, parents have a fundamental responsibility to provide for their children, but that will involve many minor decisions. The question to answer is, "Where does my duty lie?" This will take care of a surprising number of decisions.

Obedience to constituted authority. Our Lord has told us, "Give to Caesar what is Caesar's, and to God what is

God's" (Matthew 22:21). In writing to the Roman Christians, Paul said, "Everyone must submit himself to the governing authorities, for there is no authority except that which God has established. The authorities that exist have been established by God" (Romans 13:1–2). This injunction is clear, but there is one more question that calls for an answer when we face decisions: "Does this law or civic responsibility contravene the law of God?" If it does, then our attitude should be the same as that of the apostles: "We must obey God rather than men!" (Acts 5:29). *(EL)*

Focus on the Eternal

Paul had just written, "We look not at the things which are seen, but at the things which are not seen; for the things which are seen are temporal, but the things which are not seen are eternal" (2 Corinthians 4:18 NASB). For him death held no terrors because he was mastered by the powers of the world to come.

When our gaze is concentrated on the things around us—political revolution, industrial chaos, economic instability, war, crime, violence, lawlessness, the diminishing sanctity of marriage—we see much to discourage us and little to kindle optimism. But Paul exhorts us to lift our eyes and focus on eternal values. He reminds us that the Christian is not to walk according to the dictates of sight but by faith in the eternal and all-powerful God.

Peter looked at his Lord and triumphantly walked on the unstable waves. When he shifted his gaze and became engrossed with the waves, he was engulfed. When will we master that elementary lesson of the spiritual life?

For the Christian worker there are temptations to discouragement and loss of heart over the lack of visible evidence of success. We give ourselves to our task without reservation. We pray and work and sometimes weep, and yet the harvest tarries, and we tend to falter. Our wily adversary Satan plays his cards shrewdly at such times, and we sometimes fail to detect his strategy and fall into his snare.

The time factor in Galatians 6:9 is important—"at the proper time." There is always an interval between sowing and reaping. The process of germination and maturation takes time and is largely invisible. But "at the proper time," harvest is certain.

So let us not grow tired, and let us not lose heart, for "he who goes to and fro weeping, carrying his bag of seed, shall indeed come again with a shout of joy, bringing his sheaves with him" (Psalm 126:6 NASB). *(EI)*

True Greatness

All Christians are called to develop God-given talents, to make the most of their lives, to develop to the fullest their God-given powers and capacities. But Jesus taught that ambition that centers on the self is wrong. Speaking to young ministers about to be ordained, the great missionary leader Bishop Stephen Neill said: "I am inclined to think that personal ambition in any ordinary sense of the term is nearly always sinful in ordinary men. I am certain that in the Christian it is always sinful, and that it is most inexcusable of all in the ordained minister."

Ambition that centers on the glory of God and welfare of the church is a mighty force for good. The word *ambition* comes from a Latin word meaning "campaigning for promotion." The phrase suggests a variety of elements: social visibility and approval, popularity, peer recognition, the exercise of authority over others. Ambitious people, in this sense, enjoy the power that comes with money and authority. Jesus had no time for such ego-driven ambitions. The true spiritual leader will never "campaign for promotion."

To His "ambitious" disciples Jesus announced a new standard of greatness: "You know that those who are regarded as rulers of the Gentiles lord it over them, and their high officials exercise authority over them. Not so with you. Instead, whoever wants to become great among you must be your servant, and whoever wants to be first must be slave of all" (Mark 10:42–44).

At the outset of any study of spiritual leadership, this master principle must be squarely faced: True greatness, true leadership, is found in giving yourself in service to others, not in compelling others to serve you. True service is never without cost. Often it comes with a painful baptism of suffering. But the true spiritual leader is focused on the service he or she can render to God and other people, not on the residuals and perks of high office or holy title. We must aim to put more into life than we take out.

"One of the outstanding ironies of history is the utter disregard of ranks and titles in the final judgments men pass on each other," said Samuel Brengle, the great Salvation Army revival preacher. "The final estimate of men shows that history cares not an iota for the rank or title a man has borne or the office he has held, but only the quality of his deeds and the character of his mind and heart." *(SL)*

Natural Leadership Qualities

M A T T H E W   5 : 9

*N*atural leadership qualities are important. Too often these skills lie dormant and undiscovered. If we look carefully, we should be able to detect leadership potential. And if we have it, we should cultivate it and use it for Christ's work. Here are some ways to investigate your natural leadership potential:

- Have you ever broken a bad habit? To lead others, you must master your appetites.

- Do you keep self-control when things go wrong? The leader who loses control under adversity forfeits respect and influence. A leader must be calm in crisis and resilient in disappointment.

- Do you think independently? A leader must use the best ideas of others to make decisions. A leader cannot wait for others to make up their minds.

- Can you handle criticism? Can you profit from it? The humble person can learn from petty criticism, even malicious criticism.

- Can you turn disappointment into creative new opportunity?

- Do you readily gain the cooperation of others and win their respect and confidence?

- Can you exert discipline without making a power play? True leadership is an internal quality of the spirit and needs no show of external force.

- Are you a peacemaker? A leader must be able to reconcile with opponents and make peace where arguments have created hostility.

- Do people trust you with difficult and delicate situations?

- Can you accept opposition to your viewpoint or decision without taking offense?

- Can you make and keep friends? Your circle of loyal friends is an index of your leadership potential.

- Do you depend on the praise of others to keep you going? Can you hold steady in the face of disapproval and even temporary loss of confidence?

- Are you at ease in the presence of strangers? Do you shrink back in the presence of your superior? *(SL)*

More Leadership Qualities

1 TIMOTHY 3 : 6

Desirable qualities were present in all their fullness in the character of our Lord. All Christians should make it their constant prayer that they might more rapidly be incorporated into His own personality.

- Are the people who report to you generally at ease? A leader should be sympathetic and friendly.

- Are you interested in people? All types? All races? Are you prejudiced?

- Are you tactful? Can you anticipate how your words will affect a person?

- Is your will strong and steady? Leaders cannot vacillate or drift with the wind.

- Can you forgive? Or do you nurse resentments and harbor ill-feelings toward those who have injured you?

- Are you reasonably optimistic? Pessimism and leadership do not mix.

- Do you feel an overarching passion such as that of Paul, who said, "This *one thing* I do"?

- Do you welcome responsibility?

- Do other people's failures annoy or challenge you?
- Do you "use" people, or cultivate people?
- Do you direct people, or develop people?
- Do you criticize, or encourage?
- Do you shun or seek out the person with a special need or problem?

These tests mean little unless we act to correct our character or personality deficits and fill in the gaps of our training. Perhaps the final test of leadership potential is whether you "sit" on the results of such an analysis or do something about it. Why not take some of the points of weakness and failure you are aware of and, in cooperation with the Holy Spirit, who is the Spirit of discipline, concentrate on strengthening those areas of weakness and correcting faults? *(SL)*

Do You Qualify to Lead?

1 TIMOTHY 3 : 2

irst Timothy 3 spells out qualifications for spiritual leadership. With respect to relationships within the church, the leader is to be above reproach. If a charge is laid against him, it would fail, because his life would afford no grounds for reproach or indictment or wrong-doing. His adversary finds no opening for a smear campaign, rumor mongering, or gossip.

With respect to relationships outside the church, the spiritual leader should enjoy a good reputation. I knew an elder businessman who often took preaching appointments on the Lord's Day. His employees used to say that they could tell when he had been preaching on Sunday because of his ill-temper on Monday, perhaps due to the extra work of preparation. Those outside the church can see plainly when our lives fall short of our testimony. We cannot hope to lead people to Christ by living an example of such contradiction.

Outsiders will criticize; nonetheless, they respect the high ideals of Christian character. When a Christian leader full of high ideals lives a holy and joyful life in front of unbelievers, they will want a similar experience of the benefits. The character of the elder should command the respect of unbelievers, inspire their confidence, and arouse their aspiration. Example is much more potent than precept.

Moral principles common to the Christian life are under constant, subtle attack, and none more so than sexual faithfulness. The Christian leader must be blameless on this vital point. Faithfulness to one marriage partner is the biblical norm. The spiritual leader should be someone of unchallengeable morality.

The spiritual leader must be temperate, not addicted to alcohol. To be drunk is to show a disorderly personal life. Excessive drinking is a disgrace anywhere, and much more so when it captures a Christian. A leader cannot allow a secret indulgence that would undermine public witness.

A leader must be prudent, a person with sound judgment. This principle describes "the well-balanced state of mind resulting from habitual self-restraint"—the inner character that comes from daily self-discipline. The ancient Greeks, who valued this quality, described it as a disciplined mind not swayed by sudden impulse or flying to extremes. Christian leaders who possess sound minds have control of every part of their personality, habits, and passions. A well-ordered life is the fruit of a well-ordered mind. The life of a leader should reflect the beauty and orderliness of God. *(SL)*

The Likeness of Christ

"But we all . . . beholding as in a mirror the glory of the Lord, are being transformed into the same image from glory to glory, just as from the Lord, the Spirit" (2 Corinthians 3:18 NASB). Transformation into the likeness of Christ is not the result of painful striving against the bad things that captivate the heart but the result of a yearning desire for the glory of the Lord. This was the most important aspect in the new covenant of which Paul is speaking in this chapter. The old covenant only brings about deeper despair, but the new covenant holds out the attractive possibility of an attainable likeness to Christ.

The transformation begins with an objective vision of the glory of the Lord, not with mere subjective introspection. But where may this captivating vision be seen? Not in the illuminated heavens, but in the illuminated mirror of the Word. There we see reflected "the glory of God in the face of Jesus Christ" (4:6 KJV). The glory is, of course, His attributes of character and conduct and His revealed divinity. The Jews saw the face but missed the glory because of the veil of prejudice and disobedience. The vision comes as the reward of prolonged contemplation and prayer.

The objective vision of Christ results in a subjective transformation—"we are being transformed." God is not satisfied with us as we are, nor are we satisfied with ourselves. His purpose is to refashion us in the image of the Son in whom He found such delight. We have no inherent glory, but this transformation will make us reflectors of His glory. God's plan is not for a mere outward imitation of Christ but inward transformation into His image. Moses' face reflected God's glory, but the glory was external and transient. This is an ever-increasing glory that we internalize and keep for eternity.

Who is the transforming agent? "The Lord, the Spirit." The change is not automatic—our part is to steadfastly gaze on Christ as He is revealed in Scripture and to exercise an expectant faith in the Spirit's operation. He affects the change. As we meditate on our beloved Lord, coveting the beauties of His character, the Holy Spirit is working in us the virtues and graces that dwell in fullness in Him. Beholding Him, we are changed. *(CC)*

The Call to Courage

eaders require courage of the highest order—always moral courage and often physical courage as well. Courage is that quality of mind that enables people to encounter danger or difficulty firmly, without fear or discouragement.

Paul admitted to knowing fear, but it never stopped him. "I came to you in weakness and fear, and with much trembling," he reported in 1 Corinthians 2:3, but the verb is *came*. He did not stay home out of fear for the journey. In 2 Corinthians 7:5, Paul confesses that he experienced "conflicts on the outside, fears within." He did not court danger, but never let it keep him from the Master's work.

Martin Luther was among the most fearless men who ever lived. When he set out on his journey to Worms to face the questions and the controversies his teaching had created, he said, "You can expect from me everything save fear or recantation. I shall not flee, much less recant." His friends warned of the dangers; some begged him not to go. But Luther would not hear of it. "Not go to Worms!" he said. "I shall go to Worms though there were as many devils as tiles on the roofs."

When Luther appeared there before the court of Emperor Charles V, he was shown a stack of his writings and called upon to recant. Luther replied, "Unless I can be instructed and convinced with evidence from the Holy Scriptures or with open, clear, and distinct grounds of reasoning, then I cannot and will not recant, because it is neither safe nor wise to act against conscience." Then he likely added, "Here I stand. I can do no other. God help me. Amen!" A few days before his death, Luther recalled that day. "I was afraid of nothing: God can make one so desperately bold."

Not everyone is courageous by nature. Some people are more naturally timid than Luther. But whether we are bold or reticent, God calls leaders to be of good courage and not to capitulate to fear. Such a call to courage would be rather pointless if nobody feared anything. Because fear is a real part of life, God gives us the Holy Spirit, who fills us with power. But we must let that power do its work, and not fear. *(SL)*

A Leader's Humility

Humility is the hallmark of the spiritual leader. Christ told His disciples to turn away from the pompous attitudes of the heathen kings and instead take on the lowly bearing of the servant (Matthew 20:25–27). As in ancient days, so today humility is least admired in political and business circles. But no bother! The spiritual leader will choose the hidden path of sacrificial service and approval of the Lord over the flamboyant self-advertising of the world.

We often regard John the Baptist as great because of his burning eloquence and blistering denunciation of the evils of his day. His words pierced and exposed the hearts of many a petty ruler. But his real greatness was revealed in one infinitely wise affirmation: "He must become greater; I must become less" (John 3:30). Here John's spiritual stature rings clear and strong.

A leader's humility should grow with the passing of years, like other attitudes and qualities. Notice Paul's advance in the grace of humility. Early in his ministry, he acknowledged: "I am the least of the apostles and do not even deserve to be called an apostle" (1 Corinthians 15:9). Later he volunteered: "I am less than the least of all God's people" (Ephesians 3:8). Toward the end of his life he spoke of the mercies of Christ and his own sense of place: "Christ Jesus came into the world to save sinners—of whom I am the worst" (1Timothy 1:15).

The spiritual leader of today is the one who gladly works as an assistant and associate, humbly helping others achieve great things. Robert Morrison of China wrote: "The great fault, I think, in our missions is that no one likes to be second." *(SL)*

An Angry Leader

EPHESIANS 4:26

Is there such a thing as an angry leader? Indeed, Jesus had this quality, and when we use it rightly, we follow Him. In Mark 3:5, Jesus looked "at them in anger." Holy anger is the counterpart to love. Both are part of the nature of God. Jesus' love for the man with the withered hand aroused His anger against those who would deny him healing. Jesus' love for God's house made Him angry at the sellers and buyers who had turned the temple into a "den of robbers" (Matthew 21:13).

Great leaders—people who turn the tide and change the direction of events—have been angry at injustice and abuse that dishonors God and enslaves the weak. Wilberforce moved heaven and earth to emancipate slaves in England and eliminate the slave trade—and he was angry! F. W. Robertson described his sense of anger on one special occasion: "My blood was at the moment running fire, and I remembered that once in my life I had felt a terrible might; I knew and rejoiced to know that I was inflicting the sentence of a coward's and a liar's hell." Martin Luther claimed he "never did anything well until his wrath was excited, and then he could do anything well."

But holy anger is open to abuse. Many who feel it allow anger to become their downfall. Bishop Butler teaches six conditions that make anger sinful:

- When, to favor a resentment or feud, we imagine an injury done to us.
- When an injury done to us becomes, in our minds, greater than it really is.
- When, without real injury, we feel resentment on account of pain or inconvenience.
- When indignation rises too high and overwhelms our ability to restrain.
- When we gratify resentments by causing pain or harm out of revenge.
- When we are so perplexed and angry at sin in our own lives that we readily project anger at the sin we find in others.

Paul argues for holy anger when he repeats the advice of Psalm 4:4: "In your anger do not sin" (Ephesians 4:26). This anger is not selfish and does not center on the pain you currently feel. To be free of sin, such anger must be zealous for truth and purity, with the glory of God its chief objective. *(SL)*

The Ape of God

It was St. Augustine who called the devil *Simius Dei,* the ape, the imitator, of God. This concept finds support in Paul's warning in 2 Corinthians: "For such men are false apostles, deceitful workers, disguising themselves as apostles of Christ. No wonder, for even Satan disguises himself as an angel of light" (11:13–14 NASB).

In Revelation 13:11 John writes, "Then I saw another beast coming out of the earth. He had two horns like a lamb, but he spoke like a dragon." The identity of the beast is clear from the context. The dragon apes the lamb. Satan imitates God. He sets up his own counterfeit religious system in imitation of Christianity.

Satan has his own trinity—the dragon, the beast, and the false prophet (Revelation 16:13). He has his own church, "a synagogue of Satan" (Revelation 2:9). He has his own ministers (2 Corinthians 11:4–5). He has formulated his own system of theology, "doctrines of demons" (1 Timothy 4:1 NASB). He has established his own sacrificial system, "the sacrifices of pagans are offered to demons" (1 Corinthians 10:20). He has his own communion service, "the cup of demons . . . and the table of demons" (1 Corinthians 10:21). His ministers proclaim his own gospel, "a gospel other than the one we have preached to you" (Galatians 1:8). He has his own throne (Revelation 13:2) as well as his own worshipers (Revelation 13:4).

So he has developed a thorough imitation of Christianity, viewed as a system of religion. In his role as the imitator of God, he inspires false christs, self-constituted messiahs (Matthew 24:4–5). He employs false teachers who are specialists in his "theology," to bring in "destructive heresies, even denying the sovereign Lord who bought them" (2 Peter 2:1). They are adept at mixing truth and error in such proportions as to make error palatable. They carry on their teaching disguised as truth, but in fact twists all that is good and holy. (SN)

Slaves Set Free

The liberation of the will from the thralldom of sin brings with it the corresponding desire for the will of God alone.

When Abraham Lincoln affixed his signature to the historic Emancipation Proclamation, every slave in the United States of America was immediately and automatically released from slavery. From the moment the ink was dry on the document, every slave was potentially free. But that did not mean that every slave immediately enjoyed actual liberty. Some masters deliberately concealed from the slaves the news of their emancipation.

Before they experienced their freedom, the slaves first had to *hear* the good news. Then they had to *believe* that joyous news, even though it seemed too good to be true. Next they had to *reckon* on the facts being true, not of slaves in general, but of themselves in particular. But they could do all this and still remain slaves. They had to *assert* their freedom and *refuse* any longer to remain in bondage to their former masters. In doing this, they could count on the whole might of the United States being behind them.

So must it be with us. We have learned from the Holy Scriptures that on Calvary Christ signed in blood drawn from His own veins an emancipation proclamation that potentially freed all believers from the dominion of sin. It now remains for us to *believe* that fact, to *reckon* it as being true in our case, and then to act on it, *refusing* any longer to be slaves of sin. When we dare to do this, we will find that all the might of the risen Son of God is on our side, and we will be free indeed. Sin will be powerless to bring us again under its sway and dominion. *(SP)*

Responsibility for the Lost

An Egyptian woman, hearing the gospel for the first time said, "It is a wonderful story. Do the women in your country believe it?"

"Yes."

Pause. "I don't think they can believe it or they would not have been so long in coming to tell us."

"So you have come at last," said a Taoist priest to a missionary as he entered a Chinese temple. In a vision he had been impressed that someday a messenger would come from a faraway land. But should he have had to wait eighteen years?

"How long have you had the glad tidings in England?" asked Mr. Nyi of Hudson Taylor.

He replied vaguely, "Several hundred years."

"What, several hundred years? Is it possible you have known about Jesus so long and only now have come to tell us?"

A Muslim woman in Bengal inquired of a missionary, "How long is it since Jesus died for sinful people? Look at me. I am old, I have prayed, given alms, gone to holy shrines, become as dust from fasting. And all this is useless. Where have you been all the time?"

Where indeed?

Way back at the beginning of the human race there is a record of God requiring from a man an account of his brother, whose blood cried to Him from the ground. It is a striking fact that Cain, the first man to shirk responsibility for his brother, was a murderer (Genesis 4:8–10). "Am I my brother's keeper?" (v. 9) is the question of one who has no regard either for the dignity of human life or the value of a human soul. We *are* responsible for our brother. *(HL)*

Dealing with Doubt

There is much we may learn from Thomas's experience about the Master's method of dealing with doubting hearts. No believer is immune to the ravages of doubt. Even after having genuinely believed, it is still possible for us to have intellectual problems. But Jesus did not exclude this doubter from the rank of the apostles. Nor did He blame him for having a skeptical disposition. The Lord did not scold him for desiring satisfying evidence on which to base his faith, for He knew it was not the unbelief of the atheist or agnostic but the doubt of a soul genuinely searching. Archbishop William Temple suggests: "Such vigour of disbelief plainly represents a strong urge to believe, held down by common sense and its habitual dread of disillusionment."

There is a world of difference between "an evil heart of unbelief" (Hebrews 3:12 KJV) and the doubts of one who is weak in faith, between arrogant unbelief and the sensitive questioning of an earnest but hesitant heart. The doubting of the latter is a regrettable infirmity, but that of the former is an affront to God.

When the unbelieving Pharisees demanded a sign, Jesus promptly refused. "An evil and adulterous generation craves for a sign; and yet no sign shall be given to it but the sign of Jonah the prophet" (Matthew 12:39 NASB). But when Thomas wanted not only to hear but also to see and feel truth, Jesus graciously met him in his infirmity.

The beatitude Jesus talked about regarding sightless faith was not suggesting gullibility. He did not endorse a belief without inquiry and consideration, but He did indicate the necessity of a leap of faith. If it were asked what Jesus meant by believing without seeing, the answer probably is not to be found with absolute demonstration of proof. In other words, it means being willing to take the final leap of faith in the risen and living Christ.

It remains to be said that, as in the case of Thomas, God overrules doubt once and for all. It was due to Thomas's unbelief that the Lord spoke of the ninth beatitude. When those who doubt do come to faith, they believe even more firmly what they once doubted. *(JL)*

The Need for Patience

Spiritual leaders need a healthy amount of patience. John Chrysostom called patience the queen of virtues. Often we think of patience in passive terms, as if the patient person is utterly submissive and lethargic. But this version of patience needs a biblical corrective. Barclay teaches from 2 Peter (where the King James Version includes the term *patience*):

> The word *never* means the spirit which sits with folded hands and simply bears things. It is victorious endurance [and] constancy under trial. It is Christian steadfastness, the brave and courageous acceptance of everything life can do to us, and the transmuting of even the worst into another step on the upward way. It is the courageous and triumphant ability to bear things, which enables a man to pass breaking point and not to break, and always to greet the unseen with a cheer.

Patience meets its most difficult test in personal relationships. Paul lost his patience dealing with John Mark. Hudson Taylor once confessed: "My greatest temptation is to lose my temper over the slackness and inefficiency so disappointing in those on whom I depend. It is no use to lose my temper—only kindness. But oh, it is such a trial."

Many leaders can identify with Taylor's struggle. But in the face of doubting Thomas, the unstable Peter, and traitorous Judas, how marvelous was the patience of our Lord!

Leaders show patience by not running too far ahead of their followers and discouraging them. While keeping ahead, they stay near enough for their followers to keep them in sight and hear their call forward. They are not so uncaring that they cannot show a strengthening sympathy for the weakness of their fellows. "We who are strong ought to bear with the failings of the weak," Paul wrote in Romans 15:1.

Those who are impatient with weakness will be defective in their leadership. The evidence of our strength lies not in the distance that separates us from other runners but in our closeness with them, our slower pace for their sakes, our helping them pick it up and cross the line.

Ernest Gordon described his father, A. J. Gordon, with these words: "Criticism and opposition he endured without recrimination."

When we lead by persuasion rather than command, patience is essential. Leaders rightly cultivate a type of persuasion that allows maximum individual decision-making and joint ownership of goals. *(SL)*

A Purpose for Each Life

believe God has an individual will for my life and for every life, but its realization depends on a true surrender of my will and your will to Him for the fulfillment of His plan as and where He sees best. He may, however, leave considerable freedom of choice within His moral will, and He may choose to overrule our acknowledged mistakes to fit in with His will, as illustrated in the parable of the potter (Jeremiah 18).

God has a plan for every life. Our circumstances are not accidental but are planned by Him. He is not aiming to produce facsimiles but to develop each personality, so He treats us not as robots but as sons. Sometimes His dealings will seem mysterious at the time, but He has promised a future explanation. Our wisdom and vision are finite, but His are infinite. Because of our limitations there will always be areas we don't understand. For this reason, we need a Guide through the maze of life. "It is not in man to direct his steps" is the dictum of Scripture. We need a guide because the disposition of events is not in our hands. And the upsurge of demonic activity in our day makes His guidance even more necessary.

God has given many promises of personal guidance. If we wish to know what kind of guide He is, we need only look at Christ, who has revealed the Father as a loving, compassionate, gracious, and forgiving God, not as an ascetic ogre whose delight is to say no! If we make a wrong decision, we are not doomed to a second-best life. He delights in giving another chance. *(EL)*

Ways to Worship

ow can I get to know better and more intimately the Christ who reveals the Father? I can know Him primarily through the Scriptures as they are illuminated by the inspiring Holy Spirit. They are rich with material to feed and stimulate worship and adoration. The Scriptures are the only tangible way of knowing Him, as Jesus Himself indicated: "You search the Scriptures because you think that in them you have eternal life; it is these that testify about Me" (John 5:39 NASB).

In the Bible, we have the full and adequate revelation of the vast scope of the divine nature. Great tracts of truth await our exploration. Great themes—God's sovereignty, truth, holiness, wisdom, love, faithfulness, patience, mercy—illumined and made relevant to us by the Holy Spirit, will feed the flame of our worship.

The devotional use of a good hymnbook, especially the sections that deal with the person and work of the members of the Trinity, will prove a great aid to a deeper, more intimate knowledge of God. Not all of us find it easy to express our deepest feelings or to utter our love to God. When we are in the place of prayer, we are painfully conscious of the poor quality of our thoughts

121

of God and the inadequacy of words to express those thoughts. God has given the church gifted hymn writers to help His less gifted children pour out their worship and praise, and we can take their words and make them our own. Many of the church's great hymns are the nearest thing to divine inspiration.

We should, however, beware of conceiving of worship as being confined solely to the realm of thought, for in Scripture it is also linked with service. "You shall worship the Lord your God, and serve Him only," were our Lord's words to Satan (Matthew 4:10 NASB). We should not separate what God has joined, in terms of worship and service. Worship is no substitute for service, nor is service a substitute for worship. But true worship must always be expressed in loving service. *(EI)*

———⟡———

Spiritual Gifts

To be filled with the Spirit is to be controlled by the Spirit. The Christian leader's mind, emotions, will, and physical strength all become available for the Spirit to guide and use. Under the Spirit's control, natural gifts of leadership are lifted to their highest power, sanctified for a holy purpose. Through the work of the now unhindered Spirit, all the fruits of the Spirit start to grow in the leader's life. His witness is more winsome, service more steady, and testimony more powerful. All real Christian service is but the expression of the Spirit's power through believers yielded to Him (John 7:37–39).

Christians everywhere have undiscovered and unused spiritual gifts. The leader must help bring those gifts into the service of the kingdom, to develop them, to marshal their power. Spirituality alone does not make a leader; natural gifts and those given by God must be there, too.

In our warfare against evil, we need the supernatural equipment God has provided in the spiritual gifts given to the church. To be used effectively, those gifts must be enriched by spiritual grace.

Often, though not always, the Holy Spirit imparts gifts that naturally fit the character and personality of the

123

Christian leader. And the Spirit raises those gifts to a new level of effectiveness. Samuel Chadwick, the noted Methodist preacher, once said that when he was filled with the Spirit, he did not receive a new brain, but a new mentality; not a new tongue, but new speaking effectiveness; not a new language, but a new Bible.

The use of spiritual gifts in the life of the Christian does not eliminate natural gifts but enhances and stimulates them. New birth in Christ does not change natural qualities, but when they are placed under the control of the Holy Spirit, they are raised to new effectiveness. Hidden abilities are often released.

The one called by God to spiritual leadership can be confident that the Holy Spirit has given him or her all necessary gifts for the service at hand. *(SL)*

The Judge Is Judged

Pilate endeavored to get the Jews to consent to Jesus' release since none of the charges against Him had been substantiated, but all to no avail. They would be appeased by nothing less than the shedding of blood. Barabbas the murderer was preferred to Jesus the sinless Son of God in terms of freedom. Jesus was declared innocent, He was scourged, clothed in purple, and crowned with thorns. Only at the end did the true charge come to the surface. "We have a law," cried the Jews, "and according to that law he must die, because he claimed to be the Son of God" (John 19:7).

At last the cowardly Pilate succumbed to their threats and delivered Him up to be crucified. Then he washed his hands, according to the Jewish custom, saying: "I am innocent of the blood of this righteous man" (Matthew 27:24 ASV). "His blood be on us, and on our children" was their fateful response. As Maclaren points out, he took his revenge by placing upon the cross the announcement that was so galling to them, "The king of the Jews."

On what legal grounds was Jesus condemned? None! He was tried six times and acquitted three times, and yet was condemned to die. The Light of the World had shone with such a searching beam that a guilty world had to try to extinguish it.

What is the importance of the trial? "It lies in the fact," says W. Robertson Nicoll, "that the issue raised was Christ's claim to be the Son of God, the Messiah of Israel, and a King. He was tried unfairly and judged unjustly, but the true issue was raised. He died, then, because before the Jews He claimed to be the Son of God and the Messiah, and before Pilate to be Christ and King."

All generations since have felt that the judged was the Judge. The men were really standing before the judgment seat of Christ, and they all appeared with their many failings as contrasted with the Light of the World. *(31 Days)*

The Value of Prohibitions

We must by diligent study of the Scriptures and by thought and prayer arrive at our own convictions and not weakly adopt those inherited from others.

We should, nonetheless, guard against the idea that there is no place for taboos and prohibitions in the Christian life. They are plentifully found in both Old and New Testaments—the Ten Commandments, for example. If it be objected that we are "not under law but under grace" (Romans 6:15) and that the restrictions of the law do not apply to Christians, the answer is that nine out of ten commandments in the Decalogue are reiterated in the New Testament, where their application is greatly widened. Murder in the act is traced to hatred in the heart. It is true that we are no longer "under the law" as a way of justification but we are "under . . . law to Christ" as a new way of life. Paul is as strong in his prohibitions as with his calls to freedom. "Put off," "abstain," "lay aside" are characteristic commands of his letters.

The Bible does not legislate in detail for every matter of conduct that might arise, but it does enumerate clear principles which, correctly applied, cover every conceivable case. If God did not give clear guidance, how can we then be held responsible for failure to do His will? It is within the unique qualities of New Testament Christianity that lay down clear guiding principles rather than imposing a set of taboos, a system of rules and regulations, for God delights to deal with His people as adult sons and daughters rather than as children under a tutor. Since this is the case, in reading the Scriptures we should constantly ask, "What are the spiritual principles put forth in this passage?" *(SC)*

Christ in Paul

Paul's personality was not obliterated because Christ lived inside him. "I live," he said, "yet not I, but Christ liveth in me" (Galatians 2:20 KJV). He did not become any the less Paul because he was indwelt by Christ. Indeed, he became more and more the Paul God intended him to be; the ideal Paul who was a chosen vessel to the Lord. We need not fear the fullest surrender to Christ, for He enhances and dignifies our personalities. He imparts holy qualities that are absent and brings to the surface powers in our personalities that were latent. Paul became a different Paul, but a greater and a better Paul. Apart from the indwelling and control by the Spirit of Christ, the world would probably have heard little of him. Instead, his influence has been one of the dominating features of the last two millennia.

Christ lived in Paul in the sense that from within the core of his yielded personality Christ reproduced His own gracious and radiant life. Through Paul's letters, characteristic of him and bearing all the marks of his personality, Christ was able to convey His message to successive generations of Christians.

Through constant communion with Christ, Paul became less and less like the Saul of his persecuting days and more and more like the Christ with whom he had companionship. He lived a life that emanated from the same source, was inspired by the same ideals, governed by the same standards, and enabled by the same power as his indwelling Lord. His life indeed was grounded in someone else. *(CC)*

The Breath of God

E Z E K I E L   3 7 : 9

It was the breath of God that produced order out of chaos in the beginning (Genesis 1:2). Man became a living soul by God's breathing into his nostrils the breath of life (Genesis 2:7). Ezekiel witnessed lifeless corpses become a living army when in obedience to the divine command he prayed, "Come from the four winds, O breath, and breathe upon these slain, that they may live" (37:9 KJV).

With this in mind, let us consider the symbolic act of Christ, in which He graphically revealed to His disciples the source of their power. First, there was the twice-repeated blessing of peace (John 20:19, 21). Next, the Great Commission: "As my Father hath sent me, even so send I you" (20:21 KJV). Then the imparting of the Spirit: "He breathed on [into] them, and saith unto them, Receive ye the Holy Ghost" (v. 22 KJV), without whose aid they would be powerless to execute His commission. This was a miniature anticipation of the full-scale outpouring of the Spirit at Pentecost and teaches us a valuable lesson. It was as though He were saying, "All you have to do is to breathe in, to take the Holy Spirit I impart to you now. He is the power who enables you to fulfill my commission."

This graphic expiration and inspiration is the way the Spirit is received. The disciples breathed in what Christ breathed out. Could any illustration be as simple? On the Day of Pentecost God breathed out, and there came from heaven a sound like a rushing mighty wind, meaning breath. They breathed in, and they were all filled with the Holy Ghost. Breathing in is simply the equivalent of receiving. When we breathe in, the same life-giving qualities as are in the atmosphere come into us. When we breathe in or receive the Holy Spirit, that which is peculiar to Him becomes peculiar to us, just as when we place iron in the fire, the fire enters the iron and the iron partakes of the properties peculiar to the fire. *(SM)*

Tests of Spiritual Authority

To everyone entrusted with spiritual authority, serious tests are bound to come.

Can we compromise a principle to reach agreement? Lowering standards is always a backward step, and compromise nearly always requires it.

The epic contest of Moses and Pharaoh is a classic example of the temptation to compromise. When Pharaoh realized that Moses meant to lead the Hebrews out of Egypt, he used cunning and threats to frustrate him. "Worship God if you will," was his first concession, "but don't leave Egypt to do it." A modern equivalent would be: "Religion is okay, but don't be narrow-minded about it. No need to let religion isolate you from the rest of the world."

When that approach failed, Pharaoh tried something else: "If you must go out of Egypt to worship, don't go far. Religion is fine, but there is no need to be fanatical about it. Stay as close to the world as you can."

Yet a third attempt played on natural affection: "Let the men go and worship, and the women and children stay here. If you must break with the world, don't force such a narrow lifestyle on everyone else in the family."

Pharaoh's last attempt was an appeal to greed: "Okay, go. But the flocks and herds stay. Don't let your odd religious commitments get in the way of business and prosperity."

With clear spiritual insight Moses cut through each evasion: "Not a hoof is to be left behind," he said (Exodus 10:26). So Moses passed with honors a great test of his leadership of God's people.

All great leaders—Moses too—face the test of ambition. During Moses' absence on Mount Sinai, the people of Israel turned to idolatry, and God became very angry, saying, "I will strike them down with a plague and destroy them, but I will make you into a nation greater and stronger than they" (Numbers 14:12). What a test, from the mouth of God Himself! Instead of personal ambition, Moses showed selfless nobility, genuine concern for God's glory, and compassion for the misguided people. Not for a moment did the thought of selfish ambition for personal power enter his mind. He held on to God tenaciously. Through prayer, Moses saved the apostate nation from judgment. *(SL)*

Moral Perfection

In a letter published after his death, the poet Robert Browning cited several statements of men of learning concerning the Christian faith, and among them was this one from Charles Lamb: "In trying to predict with some friends as to how they would react if some of the great persons of past ages were to appear suddenly in the flesh once more, one of the friends said, 'And if Christ entered this room?' Lamb changed his attitude at once and said, 'You see if Shakespeare entered we should all rise; if He appeared, we must kneel.'" This was his view of the glory of Christ.

A brilliant Hindu scholar drew a similar conclusion. Disturbed by the progress of the Christian faith among his own people, he determined to do all in his power to arrest it. His plan was to prepare a book for widespread distribution highlighting the weaknesses and failings of Christ and exposing the fallacy of believing in Him.

For eleven years he diligently studied the New Testament, searching for inconsistencies in Christ's character and teaching. Not only did he fail to discover any, but he became convinced that the One he sought to discredit was who He claimed to be—the Son of God. The scholar then boldly confessed his faith in Christ.

The moral perfection of Christ impresses itself on the serious reader of the Gospels. The evangelists present the portrait of a real man who displays perfection at every stage of His development and in every circumstance of His life. This is all the more remarkable as He did not lock Himself in some secluded cloister but mixed freely and naturally with the imperfect people of His own generation. He became so deeply involved in the life of the ordinary people that His tendency to mix with sinners drew the most bitter criticism of the sanctimonious Pharisees.

And yet He seemed so ordinary that many of His contemporaries saw Him only as "the carpenter's son," a lowly Nazarene. With eyes blinded by sin and selfishness, they saw no beauty in Him that they should desire Him (Isaiah 53:2). To all except those whose eyes were enlightened by love and faith, His moral grandeur and divine glory passed unnoticed. *(31 Days)*

Seek Counsel

In my early years I had little hesitation about making decisions unilaterally, but I soon learned the wisdom of Solomon's proverb, "Make plans by seeking advice; if you wage war, obtain guidance" (Proverbs 20:18). I have learned the value of dialogue and consultation, for they stimulate thought, broaden vision, and give deeper insight into the issues at stake.

But advice is only as good as the one who gives it, so one should give careful thought to the question of whom to consult. Here are some recommended guidelines:

- Choose some mature person or persons in whom you have confidence, who will be able to give objective and biblical judgment.

- Avoid approaching someone whom you are sure will give advice along the lines you want to hear, in other words, someone who is so involved as to be likely to lack objectivity. King Ahab's experience is a warning beacon. When Ahab was seeking guidance, he consulted only the prophets who he was sure would approve his course. All four hundred of them agreed with him! There is danger in selecting counselors we are sure will not run counter to our desires.

- Beware of incompetent or inexperienced advisers.
- For a major decision, seek advice from more than one person.
- Don't avoid seeking advice from someone who might give adverse counsel. You'll benefit from hearing the negative as well as the positive side of the case.
- Consult Christian parents—and non-Christian parents, too, if they have a strong Christian ethic.
- Don't accept the advice tendered as final in reaching your decision. Check it against other factors.
- Don't allow your counselor to make the decision for you. It is for you to decide, for it is you who will, for good or ill, have to live with its results. *(EL)*

The Humble Carpenter

t is not difficult to conceive the wonder and perplexity of the angelic host who saw the great Jehovah, Creator of the rolling spheres, humble Himself to toil with saw and hammer at a carpenter's bench for eighteen years. They would see Him who made the heavens stoop to shape with His own hands a yoke for oxen.

Whatever else this act of humility signified, it meant that Jesus identified Himself fully with the great bulk of humanity, the common people. It gave common people's toil everlasting honor. It acquainted the Master with the feelings of these common people and gave Him insight into their inmost thoughts. His willingness to occupy so lowly a sphere for so long a time gives us both an example and incentive to be willing to do our common tasks joyously.

In common with all other Jewish boys, Jesus was required to learn a trade. What was more natural than that He should be apprenticed to His foster father and become the village carpenter? In this connection remember that in keeping with the custom of the times, Paul mastered the intricacies of the tentmaker's art as well as his university studies.

It is a challenging thought, and one that should be closely observed by those who are preparing for a life of service for God, that our divine Lord spent six times as long working at the carpenter's bench as He did in His world-shaking ministry. He did not cut short the hidden years of preparation. Jesus must be about His Father's business and doing His Father's will. If that will involved eighteen hidden, laborious, and tedious years, He would not give in to fleshly impatience but would obey with delight. "I desire to do your will, O my God; your law is within my heart" (Psalm 40:8). It should be remembered that in those times the trade of a carpenter was not considered dishonorable. It was a vocation from which it was still possible to become a rabbi.

The meekness exhibited by Jesus in working as a carpenter is all the more remarkable in the light of His subsequent amazing miracles. He could have dazzled the world with the display of His supernatural power. Instead, He worked as hard as any other man in order that in all things He might be "made like his brothers" (Hebrews 2:17). *(31 Days)*

Our Resurrection Bodies

wo current misconceptions about the spiritual body need correction: (a) it will be identical with the body that was buried; (b) no organic connection exists between the body that was buried and that which is raised. If these conceptions were so, there would need to be a new creation, not a resurrection. We must acknowledge the mystery here, a mystery that will be solved only in heaven.

In answering the question, "With what kind of body will they come?" Paul offered four truths, which are illustrated in the growth of a seed and in the diversity of animals and of the sun, moon, and stars.

1. What grows from the seed we sow is not altogether identical with what is sown (1 Corinthians 15:37). An acorn produces not an acorn but an oak, yet both enjoy the same type of life.
2. Each kind of seed has a distinctive, God-given body (Genesis 1:11; 1 Corinthians 15:38).
3. The fruit of the seed sown has an organic connection with the seed from which it sprang. It is

not a new creation but is the product of something already in existence.

4. There is great diversity in the bodies of the animal kingdom, as in the heavenly kingdom (1 Corinthians 15:39–41).

If the resurrection body is not organically related to the body that is sown as it dies, there can be no resurrection. That we are unable to explain this does not alter its truth. We should keep in mind that there may be other connected mysteries that are part of who we are. Medical researchers say that in a lifetime our total body substance changes about ten times, and yet our personal identities continue; we remain the same people, and our memory of past events remains unimpaired. *(HB)*

Prayer and the Will of God

ow can we know with certainty what is, and what is not, the will of God? If I do not know with certainty that my petition is in the will of God, how can I pray in faith? There must be a reasonable and satisfying answer, or God could be charged with unfairness in imposing a condition we are unable to fulfill.

It is my conviction that the answer to our questions will gradually emerge as we engage in the practice of prayer rather than while we are studying its theory. Study is, of course, necessary, but it must not be divorced from actual praying.

True prayer is not asking God for what we want, but for what *He* wants. This is implicit in the petition of the pattern prayer: "Thy will be done in earth" (Matthew 6:10 KJV); and as William Barclay remarks, it is not "Thy will be changed," but "Thy will be done." Prayer is not a convenient method of getting one's own way or of bending God to one's desires.

Prayer is the means by which our desires can be redirected and aligned with the will of God. As we expectantly pray for light concerning the will of God on any matter, if our desires are not in line with His will, He will

143

make it clear. If we are willing, He will change and redirect our desires, as Paul assures us: "It is God who is at work in you, both to will and to work for His good pleasure" (Philippians 2:13 NASB).

We must not imagine that God will indiscriminately grant anything we desire. What would happen in the world if this were the case? What chaos! The farmer prays urgently for rain to save his crops on the same day that the vacationer earnestly prays for sunshine. People in Britain pray in time of war for the success of their armies, while the Germans are praying for victory for their troops. God cannot grant both requests.

How are we to pray in such situations? Only one prayer is appropriate: "Lord, we do not know what to pray for as we ought; may thy will be done on earth in this matter as it is done in heaven" (see Romans 8:26 and Matthew 6:10). *(PP)*

Retirement Opportunities

GALATIANS 5:22-23

Retirement can bring unexpected and rewarding opportunities to those who take advantage of them. To those who are unprepared, they will be few, but for the enthusiastic soul, exciting opportunities of service will not be lacking. They may be in another area than one's past career, but that will only add motivation and interest.

The limitations inherent in the aging process are largely in the area of physical activity rather than of the mind. The emphasis may now shift from *doing* to *being,* but the latter is not less important than the former. That emphasis is not always welcomed by those who are by nature active.

It is noteworthy that whereas the active side of living receives prominence in the New Testament, even greater stress is laid on its passive aspects, that is, on *becoming,* not only on *doing.*

The beatitudes of Matthew 5:3–11 are largely passive in nature. The same is true, in the main, of the qualities of love enumerated in 1 Corinthians 13. The manifestations of the fruit of the Spirit in Galatians 5:22–23 are mainly passive, and each of them can flourish even in the life of a person paralyzed from the neck down, unable to move a muscle. This should say something profound to us.

Old age provides excellent soil in which the Holy Spirit can produce those attractive graces and thus prepare us for heaven, while making us more pleasant to live with on earth. In this realm there is still the possibility of endless growth.

"The influence of a Christian in old age is one of cumulative and peculiar power," says an old writer. "It gathers into itself the forces of long-tried character, and is rich in ripened experience. The work which a Christian does in the closing years of life often has a spiritual vitality in it which busier earlier years had not." True, a retiring Christian may have to vacate the seat of power but in exchange can ascend the throne of wisdom.

It is important to learn early, preferably long before retirement, how to redirect the current of life into new channels of interest and activity so that retirement will not catch us unprepared. There will still be room for ambition, but it may require redirection into other avenues. Paul's driving ambition did not wane with the passing years. The danger for those who during working life had few secondary interests is that they may lapse into inactivity and idleness. That must be guarded against at all costs. *(EY)*

The Location of Heaven

Heaven is not a material place that we can locate from down here on earth. The only clue we have as to its whereabouts was given by Jesus when He said to the disciples, "I will come back and take you to be with me that you also may be where I am" (John 14:3). Heaven is thus where God is.

Heaven is not *up* in a spatial sense, but the language used conveys the thought that it is infinitely higher than anything we know. In His human nature, Jesus could reveal this sublime truth only in terms that we could understand.

So, to the question, "Is heaven a place?" the answer is yes and no. It is not a place in the material sense in which, for example, Jerusalem is a place. It will be fundamentally different from our present, space-time environment. To Jesus, heaven was where His Father has His home.

But even this constitutes a problem, for "God is spirit" (John 4:24). Therefore He does not occupy space as we know it. He has no bodily form. Would this not imply that heaven is a state rather than a place?

We, however, are not spirit as the Father is. We will have spiritual bodies. Jesus, too, continues to have His resurrection body, which is somewhere. This would seem to require location.

In the Lord's Prayer is the petition, "your will be done on earth as it is in heaven" (Matthew 6:10). This, too, would suggest that heaven has a locale, as does the earth (Luke 15:7).

The ascension of Christ, then, suggests that heaven is a real place. He went somewhere, but the only way in which this place can be described is by the aid of biblical symbols. While heaven is not an actual city, it is like a city. All we can say with assurance is what the Bible says it is like in all its beauty and splendor and what negative earthly features will be absent from it. *(HB)*

Responsibility to Witness

M A T T H E W   2 8 : 1 9

"Therefore go and make disciples of all nations, baptizing them in the name of the Father and of the Son and of the Holy Spirit" (Matthew 28:19). How urgent is our responsibility to make the good news known to all men and women as speedily as possible? To have the knowledge of Christ and His salvation gives us an inescapable obligation to share that knowledge with everyone, as far as lies in our power, and without delay. The harvest does not await the convenience of the farmer.

It has been wisely said that even if we were academically uncertain about the probable fate of those who have never heard about Christ, the parable of the lost sheep gives us reason to act. It lays down the principle that if we are convinced of the fate of as little as one percent of humanity, we are under obligation to seek the lost, even at utmost peril to ourselves, that they might share with us in the bliss of heaven. Our responsibility for the salvation of the heathen will be as great as our ability and opportunity to give them the gospel or to make it possible for the gospel to be brought to them.

I was moved many years ago when I met a little old woman in the Philippines. She was the first convert in her village, and she had opened her heart to Christ almost as soon as she had heard the gospel.

When she was being baptized, the man who was conducting the service asked her, "Do you believe that Jesus Christ died on the cross to atone for your sins?" She gave an affirmative answer.

"And do you believe that He rose again from the dead?"

"Of course I do," she replied, "And wouldn't I have believed sooner if you had come sooner?"

How many such potential disciples of Christ are waiting for someone to bring him or her the good news of a Savior's love? Have you seriously faced your personal responsibility in this regard? *(HB)*

The Passover Song

At the feasts of Passover, Pentecost, Dedication, and Tabernacles, part of the ritual was the singing of Psalms 113–118, which were originally one song. Together, those psalms were known as the *Hallel,* a term meaning "to praise." It was the practice to divide the group of hymns into two parts, one of which was repeated in the middle of the banquet, the other reserved until the end.

Jesus found the joy of doing His Father's will so utterly satisfying that, with clear knowledge of what lay ahead, He was able to sing with insight, "This is the day the LORD has made; [I will] rejoice and be glad in it" (Psalm 118:24). Although He knew that in a few hours His Father's face would be averted from Him because of His identification with the sin of the world, He still sang, "Give thanks to the LORD, for he is good; his love endures forever" (Psalm 118:29).

Not many days before, a remarkable demonstration had taken place when Jesus entered Jerusalem sitting on a donkey. "A very large crowd spread their cloaks on the road, while others cut branches from the trees and spread them on the road. The crowds that went ahead of Him and those that followed shouted, 'Hosanna to the Son of

David! Blessed is he who comes in the name of the Lord! Hosanna in the highest!' When Jesus entered Jerusalem, the whole city was stirred and asked, 'Who is this?' The crowds answered, 'This is Jesus, the prophet from Nazareth in Galilee'" (Matthew 21:8–11).

As He sang these words, He was anticipating that in a few hours the adulation of the crowd would turn into the sullen roar "Crucify Him!" Even that did not quench His song.

Not only did He go to the cross with a song on His lips, but the last words of the song were words of thanksgiving: "Give thanks to the LORD, for he is good; his love endures forever" (Psalm 118:29). With these words, amid the shadows cast by the Passover moon, He led the little band to the olive garden.

What can we learn from the Passover song? We learn that we can turn our trouble into treasure and our sorrow into song. We can sing the song of faith in the darkest hour. Sorrow and singing are not incompatible. *(31 Days)*

Rich Yet Poor

"We know the grace of our Lord Jesus Christ, that, though he was rich, yet for your sakes he became poor, that ye through his poverty might be rich" (2 Corinthians 8:9 KJV). We are presented here with a striking antithesis—the unutterable poverty that is ours and the unsearchable riches that are Christ's. Our deep poverty serves as a black background to display the magnificence of His riches.

In relation to what is of supreme and eternal value, we are tragically poor. Our poverty may not be financial, but money is the lowest form of riches. The true value of life cannot be calculated in dollars and cents. Indeed, money has a subtle way of distracting us from what is most precious in life. The highest riches are not material but moral and spiritual, and our assets in this latter realm are pitifully meager.

What riches does Christ possess? He is heir of all things. He shared the glory of the Father. He was one with Him in a relationship of unbroken harmony. To be loved is one of life's richest experiences, and Christ enjoyed the infinite love and intimacy of the Father and of His holy angels. He said, "Thou lovedst me before the foundation of the world" (John 17:24 KJV), and His capacity to enjoy that love was infinite. How rich He was!

But "for [our] sakes he became poor," and how poor compared to His former stature! In His incarnation, He exchanged heaven's purple robes of royalty for a peasant robe; His Father's love for the illogical hatred of people. He relinquished heaven's harmony for earth's strife. He was denounced as a glutton, a drunkard, and a demon-possessed man. In heaven they cried, "Holy, holy." On earth it was, "Crucify, crucify!" Once He had been daily His Father's delight, now His Father's face was turned away. Once He had created unnumbered worlds; now He bowed His head and dismissed His spirit on the cross.

His poverty ensures our spiritual enrichment with the outcome of eternal life. Paul was writing to Corinthian Christians who were far from perfect when he said, "that [you] through his poverty might be rich." It would have been wonderful to receive a few crumbs from His table, but He makes us joint heirs with Himself. What wonderful grace from our wonderful Lord! *(CC)*

Yes and Amen

"For all the promises of God in him are yea, and in him Amen, unto the glory of God by us" (2 Corinthians 1:20 KJV). A promise of God is an undertaking by God that He will or will not do a certain thing. A promise is to be distinguished from a fact. We believe God's declared facts and claim the fulfillment of His promises. When God's Word states a fact, we take Him at His word and rest our souls on it. When He makes a promise, we comply with its conditions and expectantly claim its performance. "Where two or three are gathered together in my name, there am I in the midst of them" (Matthew 18:20 KJV) is not a promise to claim, but a fact to believe.

The Bible is a vast treasure-house of promises—thirty thousand of them, someone has calculated. But how few of them we claim for others and ourselves! They are a great bunch of keys opening every locked blessing, for they cover the whole range of human experience. There is an appropriate promise for every need. The value of a banknote depends on the integrity and resources of the bank. The worth of God's promises is vouched for by the character, integrity, and past performance of God, in whom there is no deception. With Him, promise and even-

155

tual performance are inseparable. "Hath he said, and shall he not do it?"

It is possible for us to devalue the promises of God and equate them to the level of our past experience, and so to come short of them. Our past experience is often based upon our own lack of faith or failure to fulfill our part. Or we can stagger at the promises of God through unbelief. Only through faith can we obtain the promises, for faith is the power that converts promise into performance. When God gives His promise, that is His yes. To this we give our amen. *Amen* is our endorsement of God's promises. I say amen to the signatory of a check when I present it at the bank for cashing. It is a disappointment to God if we respond to His sure yes with a hesitant amen. *(CC)*

Prayer and Predestination

Another question naturally arises as we face the problems involved in intercession. How can we reconcile intercessory prayer with the doctrine of predestination? The crux of the problem probably lies in our wrong or inadequate understanding of that doctrine. But the question is sometimes put, "If God has already predetermined all that is going to happen, how can our praying make any real difference? Would a later rearrangement of events involve God in inconsistency or contradiction?"

This is a knotty problem that has exercised the minds of praying people in all ages, and different Christians have arrived at different conclusions. The most one can hope to do is to offer a suggestion that may at least give a little help. Since God has commanded us to pray, prayer must form part of His overall purpose. Since He has pledged Himself to answer these prayers, is it not reasonable to assume that in His scheme of things He has made full allowance for all the implications of prayer? Could it not be that our prayers form part of His plan and purpose and indeed be the very factor that would bring that purpose about? If the foreordination of God is a valid objection to intercession, could it not also be contended that it is a valid objection to every other form of human activity?

In prayer we deal directly with God, and with others only in a secondary sense. The goal of prayer is the attention of God. It is not our prayer that moves people, but the God to whom we pray. Prayer influences people by moving God to influence them. If a scheming Jacob could be entrusted with power with God and people (Genesis 32:28), may we not, despite our failures, be entrusted with a similar ministry? *(PP)*

Growing in Wisdom

esus advanced in mental capacity. "Jesus grew in wisdom" (Luke 2:52). He was not an adult infant. He acquired the power of speech as did other children. He gradually gained familiarity with the ordinary branches of human knowledge. He learned to read (Luke 4:17) and write (John 8:6–8). His knowledge came to Him by degrees, but every degree of growth was perfect.

So body and mind developed together, and He displayed manly vigor and mental prowess. It is impossible to penetrate the mystery of His gradual development, but Scripture asserts it as a fact.

Although the Gospels shed no light on the education of Jesus, it is possible to gain some knowledge from the customs of the day. His first instruction was at the knee of His mother. She would teach Him to chant psalms and would instruct Him in the basics of the Hebrew law and history. From the preparations for the Passover festival, He would be told the story of redemption in the Old Testament.

In a Jewish village the size of Nazareth there would be a school, known as "The House of the Book," to which Jesus would be sent at the age of six. The rulers of the synagogue were the teachers. Up to the age of ten, the Old

Testament Scriptures were the only textbook. For five years the children memorized the Old Testament (Deuteronomy 6:7), especially the Pentateuch, until "the Jew knew the Law better than his own name." From His familiarity with the Scriptures, there was probably a copy of the sacred scrolls in the home.

The first book to be studied was Leviticus. What were the thoughts that jostled in the mind of the eager young scholar as He read the ritual of sacrifice that foreshadowed the sacrifice of God's Lamb? James Stalker remarks that no stain of sin clouded His vision of divine things, and His soul would have inklings, growing to convictions, that He was One in whom their predictions were destined to be realized. *(31 Days)*

Time and Eternity

Is time found in the ticking of the clock or the moving of a shadow? Calendars and clocks are only mechanical means by which we record our consciousness of time, not time itself. As we commonly use the word it means "duration" or "a stretch of duration in which things happen." But perhaps the most helpful definition of time is "duration turned to account." Dr. John R. Mott viewed time as our lives measured out for work, the measure of the capacity of our lives to complete His tasks.

Paul counseled the Ephesian believers to "redeem the time," or as Weymouth renders it, "buy up the opportunities," for time is opportunity. Note that time becomes ours by purchase—it has to be redeemed, or bought. We exchange it for certain occupations and activities, important or otherwise, and this is where the importance of a planned life comes in. When we say we don't have time, it may only be that we do not know how to make use of the opportunity time affords us. Time is a God-given stewardship for which we must render account, and our use of it will determine the value of our contribution to our day and generation.

The difference between one person and another is found largely in the use of time. "All attainments and achievements are conditioned by the full use of time," wrote a master of that art. "If we progress in the economy of time, we are learning to live. If we fail here, we fail everywhere. No man is or does more than his time allows him to do." In his *Holy Living*, Jeremy Taylor wrote: "God hath given to man a short time here upon earth and yet upon this short time eternity depends. No man is a better merchant than he that lays out his time upon God."

The solemn thing about time is, of course, that it can be lost, and time lost can never be regained. It cannot be hoarded; it must be spent. It cannot be postponed; it is irretrievably lost. How supremely important, then, that we make full use of the time allotted to us for the fulfillment of our life purpose! *(SC)*

Paul's Thorn

est I should be exalted above measure . . . there was given to me a thorn in the flesh, the messenger of Satan to buffet me" (2 Corinthians 12:7 KJV). In this brief biographical glimpse, Paul shares one of his deepest spiritual experiences. For this we can thank the opponents in the Corinthian church, who challenged his apostleship and compelled him to defend himself (v. 11). Robert Louis Stevenson, though a very sick man, wrote: "I should think myself a trifler and in very bad taste if I introduced the world to these unimportant privacies." Paul exercised a similar restraint, and it was only the necessity of vindicating his authority that compelled him to share a deep spiritual experience.

Paul tells of being "caught up to paradise," the realm where God is fully manifested and where he heard "things that man is not permitted to tell" (v. 4). But such an ecstatic experience included its own dangers for him, dangers with which God had His own method of dealing with Paul. He was in peril of succumbing to spiritual pride, which is clear from his own statement. Few things tend to inflate people with a sense of their own importance more than the possession of great gifts of intellect or the enjoyment of unusual experiences; and nothing more surely disqualifies them in God's service. So God brought into Paul's life an equalizing factor, so that his ministry would not be limited. "There was given to me a thorn."

We should be grateful to Paul for his reluctance concerning the nature of this thorn, which is not the main point of his disclosure. Instead, he concentrates on the unchanging principles involved. His was a representative case from which believers of all time could draw strength. *Thorn* conveys the idea of a painful stake on which he was impaled. It was something deflating in its effect, and something Satan could exploit. Satan intended it for ill, but God meant it for good.

Our thorn may be some physical disability, some temperamental weakness, some family sorrow; but whatever it is, instead of being a limiting handicap it can be a heavenly advantage. Despite Paul's thrice-repeated prayer, God did not remove the thorn. Instead, He promised compensating grace, "My grace is sufficient for thee" (v. 9 KJV). Paul accepted this grace, and his strength was made perfect in weakness. *(CC)*

Warfare and Weapons

"Though we walk in the flesh, we do not war according to the flesh, for the weapons of our warfare are not of the flesh, but divinely powerful for the destruction of fortresses" (2 Corinthians 10:3–4 NASB). The reality of the spiritual battle, of which we are very aware on a daily basis, proves the existence of Satan. The fierceness of the fight demonstrates the power and tenacity of the foe.

The warfare is spiritual, not waged in the flesh but conducted on the spiritual level; this is in a different realm from where the unregenerate person lives. It is *intangible* warfare, not with physical weapons. We cannot seize people and drag them from Satan's grasp. We can reach and deliver them only through spiritual tactics. It is a battle of two armies with entirely different goals.

It is also *interminable* warfare. The war that began in Eden will end only when Satan is finally bound. In the meantime, he is struggling unceasingly to gain control of the world and its inhabitants. There is no escaping the effects of this warfare.

The battlefield is the human mind, in our imaginations and thoughts (v. 5). Battles always have their focal points, and this war is waged in the realm of our thoughts. *Imag-*

ination, in this instance, means speculations apart from God for our own benefit. The imagination in this unhealthy sense is the source of a great deal of our sin. It conjures up wrong images and desires, and when the will entertains instead of rejects them, the citadel falls. *Thoughts* include our independent plans and purposes. The thoughts and purposes of the unregenerate man are contrary to those of God.

The invincible weapons at our disposal are the cross and the Word of Truth. "They overcame him by the blood of the Lamb, and by the word of their testimony" (Revelation 12:11 KJV). We need to use them both in the power of the Spirit. *(CC)*

The Model Prayer

The true spirit in which prayer is to be offered to God is exemplified in the Lord's Prayer. We are to pray in an unselfish spirit. It is "Our Father," not "My Father." Ours is to be a childlike spirit, the approach of a son or daughter to a father. The prayer is to be offered in a reverent spirit: "Hallowed be thy name"; in a loyal spirit: "Thy kingdom come"; in a submissive spirit: "Thy will be done in earth"; in a dependent spirit: "Give us this day our daily bread"; in a repentant spirit: "Forgive us our debts"; in a forgiving spirit: "As we forgive our debtors"; in a humble spirit: "Lead us not into temptation but deliver us from evil"; in a triumphant spirit: "Thine is the kingdom, and the power"; in a hopeful spirit: "[Thine is] the glory, for ever."

The prayer embraces every relationship. Child and father: "Our Father"; worshiper and God: "Hallowed be thy name"; subject and king: "Thy kingdom come"; servant and master: "Thy will be done"; beggar and benefactor: "Give us"; pilgrim and guide: "Lead us."

There is a beautiful symmetry in its structure. It starts with an invocation and concludes with a doxology; between these are six petitions. The first three are directed

167

godward and for His glory; the last three are human-directed and concern our need.

There is a missionary slant to the prayer. As we use it in our quiet time, we will ask that His name may be hallowed throughout the whole world. We will pray that His kingdom will know no frontiers. We will petition that His will may be done throughout the whole earth.

This is the model of the way in which we are to pray, rather than the exact form we are to use. It is capable of endless expansion. Is anything excluded from it that would add to God's glory or would more completely meet a person's need? As we pray in this way we have the glorious assurance that our Father who sees in secret will reward us openly. *(BB)*

The Supremacy of Love

"And I show you a still more excellent way . . . If I . . . do not have love, I am nothing" (1 Corinthians 12:31; 13:2 NASB). Sin may be defined as missing the mark, transgressing the law of God, or lack of conformity to the moral law of God. But in 1 Corinthians 13, the great classic chapter on love, we are presented with another conception. The standard of what we ought to be is not the Ten Commandments but the perfect character of Christ, who was the image of the invisible God. Sin includes anything in which we fail to conform to the perfection of Christ and especially failure to love God and our neighbor.

In his letter, Paul deals with failure and sin in the Corinthian church, and this wonderful chapter is one of the instruments he uses. "The beautiful lyric is thus the lancet," said James Moffatt. And a lancet is used for probing a sore and allowing the offensive pus to drain away. Each quality of love mentioned here is the perfect answer to some infection of sin in the Corinthian church—and in us too. For example, envy is the fault of those who feel inferior, and boasting the fault of those who consider themselves superior. Love is the answer to both sins—and to every other sin too.

169

In the dazzling light of this love, unworthy motivation is exposed, hypocrisy unmasked, and insincerity unveiled. The chapter forms a beautiful portrait of the life of Christ. Substitute *Christ* for *love* in verses 4–8 and note how perfectly every quality of love is matched in His matchless character. But try the experiment of substituting *I* for *love*. Can you not feel the sharp stab of the lancet? Paul contrasts love with the charismatic gifts so prized by the brilliant Corinthians and shows that they are no acceptable substitute.

If we have the courage to use this lyric on our lives as a lancet, we may find it a devastating experience, for it will probe many hidden "infections" in our lives. But the lancet is used only as a probe to a cure. What is the cure? Read verses 4–8, and substitute *Christ in me* for *love*. And Christ *is* in me. *(CC)*

The Gift of the Spirit

*N*ow concerning spiritual gifts . . . all these worketh that one and the selfsame Spirit, dividing to every man severally as he will" (1 Corinthians 12:1, 11 KJV). God has given us two unspeakable gifts—His Son and His Spirit. One is the source of our salvation, the other the inspirer of our service.

A clear distinction, however, must be made between the *gift* of the Spirit and the *gifts* of the Spirit. The former was bestowed on the church in fulfillment of the promise of the Father and in answer to the prayer of Christ. The latter are given to individual believers as and when the Holy Spirit in His sovereignty chooses.

On the Day of Pentecost, fifty days after the crucifixion, the great gift of the Spirit was poured on the waiting Jewish Christians. Later in the house of Cornelius, the Gentiles too became beneficiaries. The gift of the Spirit is for every member of the body of Christ without discrimination. The gifts of the Spirit are special and bestowed individually. The gift is absolute and permanent, but the gifts may atrophy through disuse.

Our hymnology is often faulty in petitioning God to give His Spirit, as though He had never been given. We rightly pray for a greater manifestation of His power in our lives and service, but the gift has already been made to all, once and for all.

Every believer has been granted some spiritual gift (1 Corinthians 12:11), but not all have tried to discover what their particular gift is. "Every man hath his proper gift of God" (1 Corinthians 7:7 KJV), the one most suited and essential to his function in the church. No one may demand specific gifts, for the Spirit is sovereign and gives "as he will."

A spiritual gift is bestowed apart from merit and qualifies its possessor for some form of spiritual service. There is unity without uniformity—"diversities of gifts, but the same Spirit" (1 Corinthians 12:4 KJV). Not all are clearly visible, as, for example, the gift of "helps," but all contribute to the upbuilding of the church. Some of the hidden parts of the body are the most essential.

Paul exhorts us to "covet earnestly the best gifts" (1 Corinthians 12:31 KJV), those most calculated to help and edify others. *(CC)*

Valuable Vessels

"We have this treasure in earthen vessels, so that the surpassing greatness of the power will be of God and not from ourselves" (2 Corinthians 4:7 NASB). The roots of missionary passion are concentrated in three words: *Jesus, priceless, treasure. The priceless treasure* is described in poetic language in the preceding verse: "The light of the knowledge of the glory of God in the face of Jesus Christ" (4:6 KJV). Our Lord Himself affirmed that the good news of the kingdom was a priceless treasure, but in the ultimate sense it is Christ Himself. The treasure is not a way of life to embrace but a Person to adore. But we have lost the wonder of it all. Imagine the excitement of the farmer of whom Jesus spoke, when his plow unearthed the hidden treasure! We must recapture the wonder of "Jesus, priceless treasure."

Paul sets in contrast *the contemptible vessel,* as though to highlight the contrast of such precious treasure being housed in so commonplace a vessel, yet this was God's appointed method and Christ's chosen role. He chose to share with us the limitations of our physical body, our "house of clay." That earthen vessel was the repository of "all the treasures of wisdom and knowledge" (Colossians 2:3 KJV) and "all the fulness of the Godhead bodily" (Colossians 2:9 KJV). God was pleased to display His most precious jewel in a setting of common clay. This gives a unique dignity to the vessel. Who are we to be worthy recipients of such honor?

Despite its privilege, the earthen vessel remains weak and easily corrupted. Paul knew that it was the breaking of the earthen vessel of Christ's body that enabled the full light of the knowledge of the glory of God to blaze forth to others, and the principle is the same for His disciples. It is enough to satisfy the servant that he be in the image of his Lord.

It is the strategy of God that our human weakness should be a backdrop for the display of His divine power. "The exceeding greatness of his power" (Ephesians 1:19 KJV) is to be seen as coming from God, and not from us. It is a comforting thought that God does not use us merely in spite of our weakness, but actually because of it. *(CC)*

Faith and Sight

We walk by faith, not by sight" (2 Corinthians 5:7 KJV). Two principles may govern the Christian's life: the principle of faith and the principle of sight. Sight is caught up in the material and visible; faith is occupied with the spiritual and unseen. Sight is equated with worldly prudence that guides the natural senses; faith is actually heavenly wisdom that guides the enlightened soul. Sight declares that only present things have existence; faith gives existence to future things in the next world.

These two principles are in constant conflict in each of us. There is no such thing as peaceful coexistence between them. They are mutually exclusive because they are absolutely contradictory. In each of us there is a Jacob as well as an Israel, a Simon as well as a Peter, and each ceaselessly strives to gain the victory. Before Jabbok, Jacob lived on the principle of sight; after Jabbok, he lived on that of faith. It was Pentecost that weaned Peter from sight and enabled him to live by faith.

The circumstances of life are designed to give us the opportunity to practice one principle or the other. Jacob and Esau were surrounded by the same conditions and influences, but there was a different outcome. Esau fell, but Jacob eventually stood. Jacob walked by faith, and Esau chose the path of sight, of worldly prudence.

Faith, like eyesight, has no abstract existence. It does not exist apart from the object on which it is directed. Nor is it a mere subjective state of mind. There is always an actual fact corresponding to it that gives faith substance. It is not a future hope but a present fact. Hope is expecting, faith is receiving and accepting.

Faith always involves a risk, but sight is too hesitant to take a step into the seeming void. "What if?" is not in faith's vocabulary. Faith is not faith unless we act upon it, for faith is active, not passive. On which principle are we conducting our lives? *(CC)*

Doors of Opportunity

ut I will remain in Ephesus until Pentecost; for a wide door for effective service has opened to me, and there are many adversaries" (1 Corinthians 16:8–9). When a door opened to Paul, adversaries were not excuses, but opportunities; they were not excuses for seeking an easier sphere of service, but an opportunity to rout Christ's enemies and bring more territory under His imperial banner. He laid hold of the adverse circumstances and brought them under tribute.

It would be difficult to find a more apt description of the missionary situation in the world today. There have always been many adversaries. In the early church, when persecution failed to stamp out the truth, the arch-adversary caused the Judaizers to carry the day, so that at one stage Paul was almost deserted. When the gospel overthrew paganism in Rome, Satan counterattacked by injecting a mixture of truth and error into the Roman and Greek churches. Later, when the gospel threatened to capture Africa, he succeeded in interposing Islam between Christianity and heathendom, so that these did not easily touch one another. But the last word is not with the devil, and it is the last battle of a campaign that determines victory.

Never in the history of the missionary enterprise has there been such a wide door for effective service as there is today. Some few countries have closed their doors to missionary activity at the instigation of the adversary, but they have not been able to exclude the mighty Spirit. But the majority of the countries of Asia, Africa, and Latin America often afford more strategic opportunities than ever before. These open doors are not the outcome of fortuitous circumstances but of the strategy of the Holy Spirit. But the conflict is not over when an open door is secured.

Paul sets an inspiring example. The massive difficulties of the situation, far from daunting him, constituted an irresistible challenge. "I will remain in Ephesus," where the hostilities are the most fierce. He did not seek safety in flight but attacked the adversaries and routed them. A difficulty is more than a test of our powers. It is a possible addition to our resources. *(CC)*

Ups and Downs of Leadership

LUKE 10:20

*E*very work of God includes days of frustration and days of joy. The leader is in peril of becoming overly depressed by the one and overly elated by the other. Discovering the balance here is not easy.

When the seventy disciples returned from their mission elated with results, Jesus checked their euphoria. "Do not rejoice that the spirits submit to you, but rejoice that your names are written in heaven" (Luke 10:20).

After the drama at Carmel, Elijah was so depressed that he wanted to die. The Lord corrected his self-pity in a practical manner by insisting on two long naps and two decent meals. Only then did the spiritual lessons begin, and they made a lifelong difference to Elijah. His discouragement was unfounded—seven thousand faithful Israelites had not yet bowed to Baal. By running away, Elijah had deprived this remnant of leadership they desperately needed.

Not all our ideals and goals for the work of God will be realized. People we trust will disappoint us; cherished plans will fall victim to shortfalls or sickness; the sacrifices leaders make will be interpreted as selfish gestures.

Bad things happen, but the spiritual leader should discern the reasons for depression and deal with it accordingly.

F. B. Meyer was an eternal optimist, ever hopeful, ever vigorous, ever confident of the triumph of good over evil. But as W. Y. Fullerton says, he was also "far too keen and thoughtful a man . . . not to be overcome now and again by the pessimistic views of life. He occasionally went down into the very depths of human despair. He had seen too often and too clearly the seamy side of life not to be sad and pessimistic now and then."

There are seasons when all goes well. Goals are reached, plans find success, the Spirit moves, souls are saved, and saints blessed. When Robert Murray McCheyne went through times like this, he would kneel down and symbolically place the crown of success on the brow of the Lord, to whom it rightly belonged. That habit helped save him from assuming the glory for achievement that belonged to God alone.

Samuel Chadwick wisely said: "If successful, don't crow; if defeated don't croak." *(SL)*

———

Seen and Unseen

ur inner man is being renewed day by day . . . while we look not at the things which are seen, but at the things which are not seen" (2 Corinthians 4:16–18 NASB). The renewal of the inner man must not be seen as inevitable and automatic. We are being renewed only "while we look . . . at the things which are not seen," the things visible only to the eye of faith. Preoccupation with the visible inhibits the renewal process of the inner man and dims our view of the glory to be revealed.

Concentrated attention and a steadfast gaze are needed to make the invisible real to us. If you wish to see something in the far distance, you alter the focus of your eyes. The process of renewal is operative on our behalf only as we give our undivided attention to eternal things. "Not seen," in this verse means "beyond sight" rather than "invisible," because faith makes these things real. Moses prevailed as he saw Him who is beyond visible sight. His faith brought God and eternal things into the realm of personal experience.

"The things which are seen" seem so solid and satisfying, but in reality they are illusory and transitory. It is "the things which are not seen" that are truly permanent, although they seem so ethereal. Nothing we see with our physical eye is eternal.

A pagan, Andrianus by name, deeply impressed by the fortitude of the persecuted Christians asked, "What is it which makes these Christians bear these sufferings?" "The unseen things of heaven," was the reply. This was the secret of the radiant and persevering martyrs. Because they had invisible means of support, they were neither cowards nor deserters.

It is impossible to concentrate our entire attention on the seen and the unseen at the same time. It will always be the one at the expense of the other, and we do the choosing. What is the primary focus in our lives, the seen or the unseen? Which exercises the greater influence? When we keep our gaze focused on the unseen and the spiritual, life will not be a reluctant slipping into the tomb but a glorious ascent into the immediate presence of God. *(CC)*

Preparation for Ministry

*I*f it is our unyielding purpose to overcome mediocrity and establish an effective ministry, there will be a steep price to pay. But it will prove gloriously worthwhile.

Before he was qualified to lead God's people out of Egyptian bondage, Moses had to undertake "postgraduate training." For forty years he had enjoyed luxurious living in a palace and education in Egypt's famous university. He was "educated in all the learning of the Egyptians, and he was a man of power in words and deeds" (Acts 7:22 NASB). There his intellect was sharpened and his social life polished, fitting him for ministry to the ruling elite. But God's plan for him was the leadership of a nation of slaves. For that, further preparation was needed—the time in the bleak, barren desert. In that dry university, his spirit was purified. In the unhurried solitude of his enforced isolation, he had abundant time to cultivate intimacy with God. Up until his desert experience, Moses had been an activist. Now he had to master a lesson very difficult to an activist—that *being* is more important than *doing*.

Paul had a somewhat similar experience. He pursued his academic studies under the tutelage of the famous

Jewish rabbi Gamaliel, gaining his "PhD"—Doctor of Pharisaism, someone has facetiously suggested. But though he had received superb academic training, he too had to retreat into solitude where his fiery spirit could be tempered and he could undergo the necessary theological orientation. "I did not immediately consult with flesh and blood," he claimed, "nor did I go up to Jerusalem to those who were apostles before me; but I went away to Arabia, and returned once more to Damascus. Then three years later I went up to Jerusalem" (Galatians 1:16–18 NASB). Three years alone with God in unbroken intimacy. What a preparation for spiritual ministry!

One important lesson to be learned from the experience of those men is that in training a person for a ministry, God does not shorten the training days, as we so often wish to do. For both Moses and Paul a prolonged period of solitude was an important ingredient in their preparation and a necessary part of the maturing process. *(EI)*

Death Is Not Final

delivered to you as of first importance what I also received, that Christ died for our sins" (1 Corinthians 15:3 NASB). This act takes front rank in Paul's theology. All other truths derive their meaning from this great central tenet of the Christian faith. In thinking of the cross, our emphasis tends to be too much on its physical aspects—and those were incredibly terrible—but our Lord repeatedly indicated that the bodily aspect of things was only secondary. Even death is not primarily a thing of the flesh. Jesus insisted on referring to physical and visible death as "sleep," much to the mystification of His disciples.

Of Jairus's daughter, He said, "She is not dead, but sleepeth" (Luke 8:52 KJV). Of Lazarus He said, "Our friend Lazarus sleepeth" (John 11:11 KJV). But the disciples were so obtuse that Jesus had to spell it out plainly for them: "Lazarus is dead" (John 11:14 KJV). It is clear that our concept of physical death He called "sleep." Paul follows in the steps of his Master by using His same gentle metaphor: "them also which sleep in Jesus," "them which are asleep" (1 Thessalonians 4:14–15 KJV).

Christ repeatedly declared that He came to save us from death. "If a man keep my saying, he shall never see death"

(John 8:51 KJV). Yet the saintliest soul is laid to rest in the same cemetery as the most godless. Our interpretation of death is obviously different from His.

But Christ did more than "sleep"! "He died for all." We see Him on Calvary, His face drawn in agony, His quivering body dripping blood. We hear His last gasp. But that physical cessation which we call death, He called sleep. Death meant something infinitely more terrible. Many of His followers were crucified, but they did not die—they only slept.

In Gethsemane Jesus had not begun to sleep, but He had begun to die. "My soul is exceeding sorrowful, even unto death" (Matthew 26:38 KJV). The deepening darkness, the dreadful cup, the desolation, the weight of the world's sin, and the averted face of His Father: this was *death*. He "taste[d] death for every man" (Hebrews 2:9 KJV). He died that we may never know the damning sting of death, but will be safe in His loving arms. Why should we fear the experience of physical death? It ends in glory for those who are Christ's. *(CC)*

Human in Every Sense

ur Lord's consenting to be subject to human limitations was part of the mystery of His great self-humiliation. While in His incarnate state He did not renounce His divine powers, His knowledge was so subject to human limitations that He submitted to the ordinary laws of human development. He was no exception to the rest of humanity. He acquired His knowledge through the ordinary channels open to the other boys of His day: through instruction, study, and reflection. It would appear that He even voluntarily renounced knowledge of certain future events. "No one knows about that day or hour, not even the angels in heaven, nor the Son, but only the Father" (Mark 13:32).

Like us, Jesus was not self-sustained but needed prayer and communion with His Father for the support of His spiritual life. In all the great crises of His life, He resorted not to the counsel of men but to prayer to His Father for guidance (e.g., Luke 5:16; 6:12; 9:18, 28). He was subject to human limitations of power. He obtained the power for His divine works not by drawing on His inherent deity but by depending on the anointing Spirit (Acts 10:38).

One of the strongest evidences of the reality of His humanity was His experience of human suffering. He knew the salty taste of pain. Every nerve of His body was racked with anguish. Though He was God's Son, He was not exempt from suffering (Hebrews 5:8). His sufferings of body and of spirit have formed the theme of many books. The fact that He was sinless made Him more sensitive to pain than His sinful contemporaries, for the latter deserved pain as a consequence of sin. We read of His being in agony. The events of His death on the cross assure us of His ability to sympathize with human suffering.

He displayed the ultimate in human perfections. Both friend and foe acknowledge Him as the only perfect man. All attempts to depict a perfect character in human history, other than those of the four evangelists concerning Jesus, have failed. To conceive and portray a perfect character by an imperfect author is beyond the power of fallible, sinful man.

Then how could these Galilean fishermen create such a life? The simple answer is that they did not. They merely faithfully recorded the life of One who had lived in their midst. His inner life had been open to their scrutiny as they were in daily contact with Him.

If any fact stands out crystal clear in the New Testament, it is the complete and genuine humanity of Jesus Christ. *(31 Days)*

The Cure for Loneliness

We are vulnerable to the onslaught of loneliness on a number of levels, of which the emotional area is the most distressing because it involves the loss of close relationship with other people. It can be relieved only by establishing some alternative relationships in which we need to be proactive. To those who are by nature shy or reserved, this presents an almost insurmountable obstacle.

Social loneliness is related to the contacts we have—or do not have—with the community in which we live. This is a chronic sense of being "left out," and this in turn generates a feeling of low self-worth. The victim labors under the conviction—by no means always justified—that he or she is of little significance to anyone, and therefore no one desires his or her friendship. This attitude often leads to a largely self-imposed isolation.

What people in this state of mind most need is a group of caring and supportive friends; but how and where can they find them? In many churches this need is met in home groups, whose members exercise a mutual interest in the others' welfare. But the initial step—the joining of such a group—is the decision of the lonely person.

Though social loneliness is undoubtedly distressing, spiritual loneliness is even more fundamental to the condition, for it carries with it the feeling of isolation not only from fellow men and women but also from the God who alone can fill the vacuum in our hearts.

Blaise Pascal, the noted French scientist, held that in every human heart there exists a God-shaped vacuum. Centuries before him, Augustine, the great church theologian, put his finger on the root cause of loneliness: "God created humans for Himself and our hearts are restless until they find rest in Him."

For this reason, the greatest need of the lonely person is to ensure that he or she is in a right relationship with God, the Great Physician. He has a cure for every lack and sickness of the human heart, whether it be spiritual or social. *(FL)*

Reaping the Consequences

2 PETER 2:15

Balak had heard of the fame of the prophet Balaam, so in superstitious fear he summoned him to put a curse on the Israelites and thus secure their defeat. Of course there would be an adequate reward for Balak if he succeeded.

If he were a true prophet of Jehovah, Balaam should have dismissed the proposition out of hand and sent the delegation packing back to the king. God's command was so clear and unequivocal that there were no grounds for postponing giving them a final answer. "You must not put a curse on those people, because they are blessed," (Numbers 22:12) were God's words.

But Balaam toyed with temptation, for he "loved the wages of wickedness" (2 Peter 2:15). So he left the door open for a further approach from Balak. Parleying with temptation is always fraught with danger. The serpent should be killed, not stroked.

Balak, refusing to take no for an answer, dispatched an even more prestigious delegation and promised an even more generous reward. Balaam tried to persuade the Lord to change His mind and allow him to go to Balak. When God saw that he had determined to secure the reward, whatever the cost, He went to him in the night and said, "Since these men have come to summon you, go with them, but do only what I tell you" (Numbers 22:20). It was when Balaam was on his way with the princes to King Balak that the mysterious incident of the talking donkey was enacted.

Had God changed His mind? Not for a moment. Since Balaam refused to take no for an answer, God said in effect, "If I cannot keep you from disobeying me, go, and reap the consequences." There is a limit to the divine patience with one who tries to get the best of both worlds. *(EL)*

The Perils of Leadership

God is not erratic or capricious. When we conform to "the law of the Spirit" (Romans 8:2), His infinite power is at our service. God's tomorrow of wonders depends on our today of sanctification. It is on our side that the windows of blessing are bolted shut. Our consecration withdraws the restricting bolts, and the showers are released.

If someone objects that sanctification is God's prerogative, not ours, the answer is that there is a way we must sanctify ourselves. Paul expresses it in these words: "Since we have these promises, dear friends, let us purify ourselves from everything that contaminates body and spirit, perfecting holiness out of reverence for God" (2 Corinthians 7:1).

There are some things God cannot and will not do for us, although He will supply all the power and grace necessary for a holy life. In these cases the initiative is with us. It involves, in a negative way, a putting aside—a renouncing of all that the Holy Spirit shows is alien to God's holy nature—and positively, the renewal of a complete surrender to Him and His service. When the people of Israel sanctified themselves, they renounced their sin and placed themselves without reservation at God's disposal. They counted on His faithfulness and fulfilled their own part. Amazing things soon followed. Their sanctification was the essential human factor in the resulting victory.

The order of the crossing of Jordan was to be as follows: The priests were to take up the ark and go ahead of the company, followed by Joshua and the twelve leaders of Israel, and then by the people.

At "the edge of the Jordan's waters"—God's leaders took the step of faith (Joshua 3:8). God is always loyal and faithful to the leaders He appoints, so before embarking on the campaign He honors His servant Joshua. "And the LORD said to Joshua, 'Today I will begin to exalt you in the eyes of all Israel, so they may know I am with you as I was with Moses'" (Joshua 3:7).

Exaltation to high leadership carries its own built-in perils, and not everyone survives the test. The way in which Joshua reacted to such an honor was a tribute to his humility and quality of life.

When they reached the Red Sea in their trek from Egypt, Israel had a path made for them through its waters. No demands were made on their faith. All they had to do was to walk across. Not so at Jordan. Here was no evidence whatever to their senses that the way would open up before them. They had to walk by faith and not by sight now. That is true in Christian experience. As we mature in the Canaan life, God weans us from sight and shuts us up to faith. *(PLL)*

The Weak Conscience

A weak conscience is one that is unhealthy, over-scrupulous, and oversensitive (1 Corinthians 8:7–12). It reacts faithfully according to its light, but like a compass with a weak magnetic current, it is easily influenced and tends to vacillate. Its possessor is constantly tormented by doubt as to whether an action is right or wrong and constantly digs up in unbelief what has been sown in faith.

It is very possible to become a martyr to conscience, as John Wesley discovered when he one day vowed that he would not speak to a soul unless the Spirit definitely prompted him. On arriving at Kingswood at the end of the day he found he had not spoken to a soul. He then made the resolution that when there were souls needing speaking to, it would be best for him to do the speaking and trust the Holy Spirit to use the opportunity in the best way.

A conscience may be weak for two reasons—an imperfect knowledge of God's Word and will, with a consequent imperfect faith, or a lack of surrender that leads to vacillating choices. When we obey the known will of God or are willing to do that will, we need not be harassed by an overscrupulous conscience, and we should refuse to constantly review an action committed in good faith. Too many are given to the unsatisfying occupation of photographing themselves and developing their own film. The corrective is to clearly face the issues involved in a situation in the light of Scripture and, seeking the guidance of the Spirit, come to a decision according to one's best judgment. Thereafter we should resolutely refuse to reopen the matter. *(SC)*

The Fire of God

"Now when Solomon had made an end of praying, the fire came down from heaven . . . and the glory of the Lord filled the house" (2 Chronicles 7:1 KJV). The presence of the fire was proof of the presence of God.

Such was the significance of the symbol of fire in Old Testament times. But what is its meaning for us today? In the New Testament it is symbolic of the presence and energy of the Holy Spirit. Announcing the ministry of the Messiah, John the Baptist said, "He shall baptize you with the Holy Ghost, and with fire" (Matthew 3:11 KJV). His prophecy was fulfilled. On the Day of Pentecost when the Holy Spirit came with power upon the assembled disciples, the chosen symbol was prominent. "There appeared unto them cloven tongues like as of fire, and it sat upon each of them" (Acts 2:3 KJV). There is therefore justification for the view that the symbolism of fire in its present-day application is the presence and power of the Holy Spirit.

In Elijah's day the holy fire had disappeared from the altars of Jehovah; and false fire was burning on the altars of Baal. The glory had departed, and no man could rekindle the sacred flame. When Nadab and Abihu "offered

197

strange fire before the Lord" (Numbers 3:4 KJV), they died, for there can be no substitute for the true fire of God.

In our day, the greatest lack in the life of the individual Christian and of the church is the fire of God, the manifested presence and mighty working of the Holy Spirit. There is little about us that cannot be explained on the level of the natural. Our lives are not fire-touched. There is no holy blaze in our churches to which people are irresistibly drawn as a moth to a flame. It is the absence of the fire of God that accounts for the insignificant impact the church is making on a lost world. It never had better organization, more scholarly ministry, greater resources of people and means, and more skillful techniques. And yet never did it make a smaller contribution to solving the problems of a distraught world. Our prayer should be, "Lord, send the fire." What else can meet the need of the hour? *(SM)*

If in Doubt... Question

To ask and answer the following positive questions will automatically deal with many problems concerning doubtful things.

Will it bring glory to God? "Whatsoever ye do, do all to the glory of God" (1 Corinthians 10:31 KJV). If the chief end of man is to glorify God, this should be our first test and chief concern. If the proposed course of action primarily benefits the self and does not bring glory to God, it is something that can well be laid aside.

Is it profitable? Will it help me in my Christian life, my witness, my service? "All things are lawful for me, but all things are not expedient: all things are lawful for me, but all things edify not" (1 Corinthians 10:23 KJV). Will it tend to make my life more profitable to God and to my fellow human beings?

Does it edify? Does it build me up in my Christian character, and will it help me to build up the church of God? "For edification, and not for your destruction" (2 Corinthians 10:8 KJV). God's supreme interest is centered in His church, and we should share His concern for its upbuilding.

Does it tend to enslave? "All things are lawful for me; but I will not be brought under the power of any" (1 Corinthians 6:12 ASV). Even lawful things can become our master and get out of balance. They can so demand our attention that we neglect other things of more importance. For example, secular reading can so enslave readers that it dulls their appetite for the reading of the Word of God and spiritual books. Such a condition must be jealously guarded against by strict self-discipline, both as to the quality and the quantity of our secular reading.

Will it strengthen me against temptation? It is of little avail for us to pray, "Lead us not into temptation," if we voluntarily go where we will be exposed to temptation. It is one thing for a Salvation Army officer to enter a tavern to sell his *War Cry* but quite another for a young person to go in to "celebrate" with friends. Any place or practice that tends to make sin less sinful is to be shunned. *(SC)*

God-Given Time

ur Lord moved through life with a majestic and measured tread, never in a hurry and yet always thronged by
demanding crowds, never giving those who sought His
help a sense that He had any more important concerns
than their particular interests. What was His secret? Knowing that every person's life is in the plan of God, He realized that His life and all the conditions in which it was to
be worked out were under the perfect control of His Father.

Time held no power over Him. On several occasions
He asserted that His hour had not yet come. There was
the consciousness that His Father's plan had been drawn
with such meticulous accuracy that every hour fit into the
overall purpose of His life. His calendar had been
arranged, and His sole concern on earth was to fulfill the
work given Him to do in the allotted hours (John 7:6;
12:23, 27; 13:1; 17:1). Nor would He allow His much-
loved mother to interfere with this divinely planned
timetable (John 2:4). Deep human affection could not be
permitted to affect His schedules, or His Father's plan
would be marred (John 11:6, 9).

Small wonder then, that at the close of life He could
review it with absolute objectivity and speak the self-

approving words: "I have finished the work which thou gavest me to do" (John 17:4 KJV); no part of His life was marred by undue haste or imperfectly completed through lack of time. He found sufficient time in the twenty-four hours of the day to do the whole will of God.

The Lord's corrective word to His disciples, "Are there not twelve hours in the day?" (John 11:9 KJV), seems to suggest a quiet, steady confidence in His Father's purpose and a resulting courage even in face of enemies and danger. Interruptions could not disturb His peace because they had already been provided for in the Father's planning, and the wrath of enemies would have to await His "hour." Thus He could pursue His work undisturbed, knowing it would be "finished." There would be time for all that God meant Him to do, though there might not always be "leisure so much as to eat" (Mark 6:31 KJV). *(SC)*

Prayer and Conscience

Instead of having confidence in approaching God, we may be held back by a condemning heart. John the apostle assured those to whom he was writing that whatever condemns us in our conscience hinders prayer. Until known sin is judged and renounced, we pray and plead in vain. "Beloved, if our heart does not condemn us, we have confidence before God; and whatever we ask we receive from Him" (1 John 3:21–22 NASB).

If we know of some reason our conscience condemns us, it is for us to deal with it and do all in our power to put it right with God and people. Until we do, we will endeavor in vain to pray the prayer of faith. More often than not this is why we are unable to exercise appropriating faith when we pray.

What are we to do if some subtle sense of guilt and condemnation descends on our spirits? We examine our hearts but can assign no reason for the distress. It is a nameless depression of spirit, a vague disturbance that prevents the soul from rising to God in the prayer of faith. How is this condition to be remedied?

First, let us sincerely ask God to reveal to us if there is some real but unrecognized sin that lies at the root of this sense of condemnation. If He reveals something to us, let us put it right at the first opportunity. Confidence toward God will thus be restored, and our prayers will receive their answers.

But should there be no such revelation of sin, we are justified in concluding that the obscuring cloud originates in enemy territory. Many have found it helpful to pray in such circumstances, "Lord, if this sense of condemnation comes from Your Spirit's conviction, make my sin clear to me, and I shall confess and put it right. But if it comes from Satan, then on the grounds of Calvary's victory, I refuse and reject it."

This attitude of acceptance of the divine dealing but rejection of the satanic intrusion has often brought deliverance and renewed freedom in prayer, for it is true that "if our heart does not condemn us, we have confidence before God." *(PP)*

I Must Choose

W. S. Way presents the activity of God as "supplying the impulse, giving you the power to resolve and the will to perform the execution of His good pleasure." We are not cast back upon our own resources. We have the benefits accruing from the death and resurrection of Christ and His gift of the Holy Spirit through whom those benefits become operative in our lives. But I must do the choosing. God does not impart His power or blessings apart from the active participation and co-operation of our wills. Once I put my weak will on God's side and despite my own conscious weakness choose His will, it becomes possible for the Holy Spirit to empower my will.

Even after God has supplied the right impulse, giving humans the power to choose, it still remains for them to act. God cannot act for them. Sanctification is essentially proactive; it does not consist merely in not doing evil things. In exercise of the new power imparted by God's Spirit people are now able to perform "His good pleasure"—the whole will of God. In themselves they are no stronger, but with the divine indwelling and in-working, they are no longer the victim of weakness and sin.

205

No more apt illustration of the cooperation of man with God is recorded than that of the man with the withered hand. Try as he would, no attempted exercise of his will produced any effect on the paralyzed muscles. When our Lord commanded him to stretch out his hand, a natural reaction would have been for him to say that he had attempted to do so a thousand times, without effect. Was there any reason to expect anything different the thousand-and-first time? But faith had been kindled in the man's heart, and in response to the Lord's command, he exercised his will, and to his joy the paralyzed hand responded, as whole as the other. The activity of faith had released the power of God. The physical realm was affected by the spiritual realm. "All things are possible to him that believeth" (Mark 9:23 KJV). *(BB)*

The Law of Restraint

Honest self-criticism should not lead to unwarranted criticism of others but will serve the function of helping to save us from the judgment of God (1 Corinthians 11:31).

Praying Hyde of India learned a lesson that he said was the most profound the Lord ever taught him.

He was burdened about the spiritual condition of a certain pastor and resolved to spend time in intercession for him. He began pouring out his heart for him somewhat as follows: "O God, Thou knowest this brother, how —" He was going to say "cold," when suddenly a hand seemed to be laid on his lips, and a voice said to him in a stern rebuke: "He that toucheth him toucheth the apple of mine eye." A great horror came over Hyde. He had been guilty before God of "accusing the brethren." He had been judging his brother. He fell humbly to his knees.

It was he himself who first needed putting right. He confessed his sin and claimed cleansing. "Whatsoever things . . . are lovely . . . [and] of good report . . . think on these things" (Philippians 4:8 KJV). Then he cried, "Father, show me what things are lovely and of good report in my brother's life." In a flash he remembered how that pastor had given up all for Christ and endured much suffering. He was reminded of years of hard work, of the tact with which he had managed a difficult congregation, of the many quarrels he had healed, of what a model husband he was. His prayer session was spent in praise for his brother instead of praying for change. *(BB)*

God's Enabling Power

We are not left to our own unaided human resources, dependent on our material environment. The eternal triune God dwells in us. "If a man love me . . . we will come unto him, and make our abode with him." "The Spirit of truth . . . shall be in you" (John 14:23, 17 KJV). There is surely sufficient incentive in this glorious fact to convince the believer to cooperate with his indwelling Guest with all His powers.

Not only does the omnipotent God dwell in the believer's heart, but also He is at work there, the active agent in our sanctification. "It is God which worketh [is working] in you" (Philippians 2:13 KJV) with power adequate for every need. And God's working is always effectual. How impossible it would be for us to force tons of water through solid wood! Yet every day, as the sap rises in the tree, this miracle is performed a thousand times over. With this consciousness of the divine in-working, Paul exclaimed: "I can do all things through Christ which strengtheneth me" (Philippians 4:13 KJV). The words "all things" here do not indicate in the original that he could do "all things in the universe" but implied that he could do everything that was in the good pleasure of God for him to do. Within the sphere of God's will he experienced unlimited power.

"To will and to do of his good pleasure" (Philippians 2:13 KJV). Here is another aspect of the paradox. God works within me to will and to work, and yet the willing and working are mine. But it should be noted that God does not will *instead* of me or work *instead* of me. In sanctification God and I are joined in indivisible partnership, and all efforts to separate the respective spheres of activity are in vain. I will to do, but God works the will in me. I work, but God supplies the power. *(SC)*

Responding in Service

NUMBERS 11:11

*U*ntil the very moment of his collapse, Moses had been selfless in his care of his people. Indeed, when the anger of God was kindled against the idolatrous people, Moses had asked that his name be blotted out of God's book (Exodus 32:32), if only they might be spared. But he dropped to a lower plane in Numbers 11:11–15. Forgetting the desperate spiritual need of the people, he reproached God and indulged in self-pity. He lost sight of all that God had enabled him to achieve and became self-absorbed.

Elijah, too, in his time of reaction, reproached God and in strange disillusionment cried: "I am not better than my fathers" (1 Kings 19:4 KJV). His self-esteem had been dealt a shattering blow. "I have been very jealous for the LORD God," he complained (v. 14 KJV), implying that in spite of his zeal, he had been "let down." His twice repeated, "I, even I only, am left" (vv. 10, 14 KJV), indicates his sense of loneliness in his devotion to God. He too was engulfed in self-pity.

Nor was the case different with Jonah. His cause for reproaching God was resentment of His grace and forbearance! The real trouble was that God's goodness to

211

Nineveh had shattered his reputation as a prophet. Jonah had prophesied judgment, and God had exercised mercy. Since his reputation was gone, Jonah concluded that it would be better to die than to live.

In each case the desire to die stemmed from making self and self-interest supreme instead of God and His glory. Is not all despondency in essence a manifestation of self in one form or another? *(SC)*

The True Vine

For a maximum yield, the branches of the vine need heavy pruning—heavier than most other trees. Unless it is severely cut back, the fruit will be sparse and poor. So God prunes the lives of His children, cuts back the undesirable growth of the self-life, not because He delights to see them suffer but that their lives might be increasingly fruitful. He desires to see His children growing in spiritual maturity. There is to be a progression—"fruit, more fruit, much fruit."

The abiding is to be reciprocal: "Abide in me, and I in you" (15:4 KJV). There is a conditional promise of answered prayer: "If you abide in Me, and My words abide in you, you shall ask what ye will, and it shall be done unto you (v. 7 KJV). Christ in me—I in Christ—Christ's word abiding in me. That is intimacy indeed. With His Word constantly meditated on, loved, believed, and obeyed, we will increasingly receive and reflect the mind of Christ. His will becomes ours, and our desires will be only what He desires.

The little daughter of a friend of mine one day said to her father, "Daddy, I do like to do what I do like to do!" That mutual and reciprocal abiding in Christ will mean that we will like to do what *He* likes us to do.

Abundant fruit is the proof of discipleship. "My Father is glorified by this, that you bear much fruit, and so prove to be My disciples" (John 15:8). Not all believers are true disciples, according to that statement. Our discipleship will be displayed by our abiding in His love, enjoying it, reveling in it—a love as great as the Father has for the Son (15:10). Simple obedience is a secret of abiding in His love. Mutuality of love will inevitably result in a deepening intimacy.

Abounding joy results from abiding (15:11 NASB). "I have spoken to you . . . that your joy may be made full"; in other words, "that you may share with Me the joy I possess." Our joy is inextricably linked with His. *(EI)*

Restoring Relationships

In order to restore right relationships, we may need to confess to others as well as to God, for we cannot be right with God and wrong with others.

The sincerity of our confession may need to be evidenced by *restitution*. Apology may need to be made, a quarrel settled, a debt paid, a relationship terminated, if we are to enjoy renewed fellowship with God and people.

Here arises the question of what we should confess and to whom we should confess it.

As all sin is against God, obviously we should confess to Him every sin of which we are conscious, and we should do it without delay, as soon as we realize we have sinned. Some sins are against God alone, but others are against our fellow humans and thus require confession to them.

The scriptural principle involved would seem to be that the confession should be related to the sin. Where the sin is against God alone, the sin needs to be confessed only to God. There may sometimes be therapeutic value in sharing a problem with another trusted friend, but there is no necessity to do so.

Where the sin is against a fellow person, it should be confessed to the one who has been injured by our sin, and need be confessed to no other. Nothing is gained merely by giving someone else, who is not involved, knowledge of your sin.

Where the sin is against a church or group, the sin should be confessed to the church or group in an appropriate manner, probably to the leader, who could decide what action, if any, should be taken.

What about public confession? In some cases that may be called for, but such cases would be rare. Meetings at which there is intimate public confession of personal sins should not be encouraged, as they are often definitely harmful.

On some occasions, however, especially during times of revival and under the pressure of the Holy Spirit, a person can find relief only by confessing specific sins in prayer, and I have seen that several times. But it has always been accompanied with deep humility and brokenness. Anything that savors of exhibitionism or illegitimate interest should be abjured. *(EI)*

Never Give Up

Who of us has never been tempted to lose heart? Who has not been on the point of dropping their bundle of problems and responsibilities? None of us is exempt from the subtle, debilitating attacks of our adversary on that level. Few are fortunate enough to escape periods of depression, whether as a result of adverse circumstances or the tyranny of temperament. That Paul had been no stranger to that malady of the soul is clear from his four-times repeated assertions, "We do not lose heart"; "Being always of good courage" (2 Corinthians 4:1, 16; 5:6, 8 NASB). By the time he penned that letter, he had mastered the secret of endurance and victory.

It is a strong statement, and alternative translations highlight its meaning: "We never give up." "Nothing can daunt us." "We never collapse." There must be some very strong motivation, some unusual secret of power that enabled Paul to make such a daring assertion.

"But that was the great apostle Paul," you say. "If I were Paul with his spectacular gifts of nature and of grace, his superb training, his apostolic authority, and his success in service, perhaps I would not lose heart either. But I am no Paul!"

But did everything drop into Paul's lap? Was he spared the severe testing that affects a Christian worker or beleaguers a missionary or pastor? I quickly thumbed through Paul's second letter to the Corinthians to discover the kind of circumstances over which he triumphed. Pause here and read 1:8; 2:4; 4:8; 6:4–10; 7:5; 11:23–28; 12:7. What a mounting list of trials! How trivial our burdens appear when compared to the weight of his cares.

It should be borne in mind that in those passages Paul shared with us the secrets of his victory over depression and discouragement. It is most unlikely that he reached that plane of victory all at once. He was not immune to depression, for he wrote, "But God, who comforts the depressed, comforted us by the coming of Titus" (2 Corinthians 7:6 NASB). He was not spared the difficult lessons of life. "I have learned," he wrote, "to be content in whatever circumstances I am" (Philippians 4:11 NASB). *(EI)*

Forms of Pride

*P*ride takes many forms, but spiritual pride is the most grievous. To become proud of spiritual gifts or leadership positions is to forget that all we have is from God, and the position we occupy is by God's appointment.

The victim of pride is often least aware of the sin. Three tests help us identify the problem:

The test of precedence. How do we react when another is selected for the position we expected to have or wanted to fill? When another is promoted in our place? When another's gifts seem greater than our own?

The test of sincerity. In our moments of honest self-reflection, we often admit to problems and weaknesses. How do we feel when others identify the same problems in us?

The test of criticism. Does criticism lead to immediate resentment and self-justification? Do we rush to criticize our critic?

When we measure ourselves by the life of Jesus, who humbled Himself on the cross, we are overwhelmed with the vileness of our hearts, if we are honest.

One of the repulsive manifestations of pride is egotism, which is the practice of thinking and speaking of oneself, of magnifying one's attainments and relating everything to one's self rather than to God and God's people. The leader who has long enjoyed the admiration of many followers stands in peril of this danger.

Jealousy is also a near relative of pride and describes the person who is suspicious of rivals. Moses faced such a temptation concerning the loyalty of his own followers. Eldad and Medad are "prophesying in the camp," an outraged Joshua reported. "Moses, my lord, stop them!" (Numbers 11:27–28).

But the great leader saw the situation for what it was, an outbreak of God's Spirit among the assistants Moses had selected. "But Moses replied, 'Are you jealous for my sake? I wish that all the LORD's people were prophets" (Numbers 11:29). Envy and jealousy found no fertile ground in Moses' heart. God's work in others was to be encouraged, not snuffed out. *(SL)*

Joy of Tithing

Admittedly, tithing is nowhere specifically commanded in the New Testament, since that is not the wisdom of God's method under grace. Instead of legislating regulations, Jesus disclosed principles by which His disciples were to regulate their conduct. "I am not commanding you" were Paul's words. He knew that a generous hand without a loving heart was of no value.

Tithing was practiced by the patriarchs four hundred years before the Law was given (Genesis 14:20; 28:22). The usage of consecrated tithes prevailed among Romans, Greeks, and Arabians as well as with the Jews; so tithing seems to rest on the common law of God's kingdom rather than on special Hebrew legislation.

Jesus Himself gave tithes and offerings. Is the servant greater than his Lord?

It is a misconception of the meaning of *grace* to think that it leaves an option for a believer to do less than a devout Jew would have done. If the true spirit of grace has gripped my heart, I will not be calculating the minimum I can get away with but the maximum I can give to my Lord. The New Testament standard is not lower than the Old.

In speaking about tithing in Matthew 23:23, Jesus said, "You give a tenth of your spices—mint, dill and cumin. But you have neglected the more important matters of the law—justice, mercy and faithfulness. You should have practiced the latter without neglecting the former." Did that obligation cease a few days later when He died? Is the Christian not "under law to Christ (KJV)," with His higher law of love? "I am not free from God's law," said Paul, "but am under Christ's law" (1 Corinthians 9:21).

It would seem from an impartial weighing of the relevant Scriptures that though there is no legal obligation resting on believers to give a tithe, or even more, of their income, their experience of Christ's matchless grace should provide a powerful incentive to emulate the example of their Master. The experience of sacrifice is the ecstasy of giving the best we have to the One whom we love the most. *(EI)*

God's Veto

f God should veto a certain course of action on which your heart is set, be assured that He has not done it out of caprice. It is because of His deep concern that you do not miss the best He has for you. It is the expression of His perfect wisdom and love. "God disciplines us for our good, that we may share in his holiness" (Hebrews 12:10). It is the best wisdom to wait for the gradual unfolding of God's will in providence.

Sometimes when our cherished plans are checkmated, it is not denial, only delay for some wise purpose. The experience of the Israelites immediately after their deliverance from Egypt is a case in point. From the place where they crossed the Red Sea to the borders of Canaan at Kadesh Barnea, the journey would normally take only eleven days (Deuteronomy 1:2). Taking the route they traveled, however, it took them several months.

It must be remembered that the Israelites had lived as slaves all their lives; others made the decisions for them. So God in His compassion allowed them sufficient time to adjust to their new status.

The wisdom of this detour soon became apparent. When they began to meet opposition and the going became difficult, they soon showed how ill prepared they were for the conflict and hardships that lay ahead. They desperately needed the brief but gentle initiation of the desert experience to toughen and mature them and fit them for conflict against war-experienced foes.

So does God at times lead His servants on what seems like a pointless detour. His leading crosses our desires and inclinations because He is working for eternity and has deeper purposes in view. *(EL)*

Supernatural Resources

"Give yourselves wholly to prayer and entreaty; pray on every occasion in the power of the Spirit" (Ephesians 6:18 NEB). Prayer demands more than mere human power and energy for its supernatural task, and the Holy Spirit supplies it. He is the Spirit of power as well as the Spirit of prayer. Mere human energy of heart, mind, and will can achieve only human results. But praying in the power of the Spirit releases supernatural resources.

It is the Spirit's delight to aid us in our physical and moral weakness in our prayer life, for the praying heart labors under three limiting handicaps; but in each of them we can count on the Spirit's assistance. Sometimes we are kept from prayer because of the conscious sin of our hearts. The Spirit will lead and enable us to appropriate the cleansing of the blood of Christ, which will silence the accusations of the adversary and remove the sense of guilt and pollution. We are always hampered by the limiting ignorance of our minds.

The Spirit who knows the mind of God will share that knowledge with us as we wait on Him. Then we will have the quiet, clear conviction that our request is in the will of God, and faith will be kindled. We are often earth-bound through the numbing infirmities and limitations of our bodies. The Spirit will quicken our mortal bodies in response to our faith and enable us to rise above physical and environmental conditions.

Are we receiving His help along these lines? Is this our present experience? Have we slipped into an independence of the Spirit? Are we habitually praying in the Spirit and receiving full answers to the strategic prayers He inspires? Our intellectual appreciation of spiritual truths often outruns our practical experience of their implications and benefits. *(BB)*

Giving Beyond the Limit

"It is more blessed to give than to receive" (Acts 20:35). By divine decree, what I give comes back to me in greater spiritual blessing.

An English nobleman who lay dying said remorsefully,
"What I spent, I had;
What I kept, I lost;
What I *gave* I have."

What did the early church practice in terms of giving to the church and other causes? One might have expected the wealthy, richly gifted Corinthian church to be Paul's model. Instead, it was the poverty-stricken colonial church in Macedonia, rather than in Corinth, that demonstrated and experienced the superior blessedness of generous giving (2 Corinthians 8:1–5).

They were remarkable people. In striking contrast to their deep poverty and affliction shone the riches of their abounding liberality: "That in a great ordeal of affliction their abundance of joy and their deep poverty overflowed in the wealth of their liberality" (v. 2 NASB). Despite their limited resources they did not shrink from giving to the point of costly sacrifice. They calculated the maximum

227

they could give and then went beyond it (v. 3). The question with them was not, "How little?" but, "How much?"

It is a common tendency even among Christians in our day to spend beyond the limit of our means, but have we ever emulated the Macedonians? "For I testify that according to their ability, and beyond their ability they gave of their own accord, begging us with much urging for the favor of participation in the support of the saints" (vv. 3–4 NASB).

What an extraordinary picture! The donor is the one who does the begging! The donor is the one who takes the initiative. Since they gave beyond the limit of their means, they were obviously looking to God to supply their other needs. They gave by principle, not by impulse. Their giving grew out of their surrender to Christ (v. 5).

The Macedonian Christians set us a noble example of liberality, with the result that they themselves experienced "abundance of joy" (v. 2 NASB). *(EI)*

Necessity for Preparation

In dramatic yet tender language, the prophet Isaiah brought God's message to His chastened people. " 'Comfort, O comfort My people,' says your God. 'Speak kindly to Jerusalem'" (vv. 1–2 NASB). That wooing note of love must have evoked a warm response in the heart of exiles pining for their homeland.

An assurance of pardon (40:2). First, he told them that though the nation's sin had been extreme, it had been pardoned; and her warfare, or hard service, had ended. The divine discipline had achieved its purpose, and the penalty of her iniquity had been accepted as paid off. Now the grace of God could be freely expressed toward her.

The necessity for preparation (40:3–4). Next the prophet stressed what they must do if the glory of God were again to be revealed in their midst. "Make smooth in the desert a highway for our God" (v. 3 NASB). In the East, a victorious general, returning from his conquest, was given the victor's triumphal march. History records titanic feats of engineering in making perfect roads through the trackless desert for the conquering hero. Every low place was filled, every high place reduced, every uneven place leveled, so that the conqueror might enjoy unimpeded progress.

John the Baptist referred to that custom when describing his function as forerunner of the Messiah (Matthew 3:3). But it also enshrines an important and contemporary spiritual principle. If God is to reveal Himself in special blessing to His people, there must be spiritual preparation. John's task was to create in the nation such a sense of sin and repentance as would make it possible for the Holy Spirit to work in power among them.

It must be this way among God's people today. Anything in this life must be straightened, any stumbling blocks removed. Low levels of spiritual living must be raised and rough elements of character polished. Areas of neglect must be remedied and relationships adjusted. This is something for which we alone are responsible, but the Holy Spirit will empower us to do it. *(EI)*

Midlife Stamina

Middle life has its own peculiar testings in both physical and spiritual realms. They may not be so volcanic as those of youth, but what they lose in intensity they gain in subtlety. Many who soared like rockets in their youth have descended like burnt-out sticks before the testings of middle life. Marriage has knocked many a young man and woman out of active spiritual warfare. It is at this stage that there often comes a loss of fervor and a waning of personal devotion.

A lukewarm sense of duty replaces ardent heart-love. Instead of transforming the vanishing enthusiasms of youth into a worthy life-purpose, life becomes anemic and insipid. The temptation comes to ease up on self-denial and to yield to softening ease. Unrealized ideals of unconditionally surrendered service to God are condoned and accepted as inevitable. With the toleration of compromising attitudes and habits, disillusionment, criticism, and even cynicism become the normal pattern of life. A subtle deterioration and lack of zeal unconsciously sets in. "Gray hairs are here and there upon him, yet he knoweth not" (Hosea 7:9).

Caleb passed the test of youth with flying colors, but how will he fare in the long, drawn-out years of middle life? Few have faced such a hard and potentially embittering lot at this stage of life as Caleb. The sin and unbelief of his contemporaries doomed him to a life of disappointment and frustration for the forty years that should have been the best in his life. The apparent reward of his faith and courage was aimless wandering in the desert when his powers were at their peak and his ambition at its zenith. Unbelief always involves others in suffering.

By all worldly standards, he would have been justified in self-pity and resentment, but he maintained his spiritual integrity. He survived the long-sustained test without losing stature. He was one of those rare people who was not offended with God in His dealings with him. When Moses died, it was Joshua—not Caleb—who was chosen as leader. He was not even made second in command of the army. In his heart there was neither jealousy of Joshua nor bitterness against God. *(BF)*

Ascension into Heaven

The ascension was a divine vindication of Jesus' claims to deity that had been rejected by the Jews. He had claimed the right to ascend into heaven as His own prerogative. "No one has ever gone into heaven except the one who came from heaven—the Son of Man" (John 3:13).

Finally, it was time for His divine inauguration into His heavenly priesthood, sitting at the right hand of God. For the believer, our Lord's ascension has blessed implications for us. Though physically remote, He is always spiritually near. Now that He is free from earthly limitations, His life above is both the promise and the guarantee of our life to come. "Because I live, you also will live," He assured His disciples (John 14:19). His ascension anticipates our glorification and leaves us the assurance that He has gone to prepare a place for us (John 14:2).

His resurrection and ascension to heaven involved nothing less than making His humanity eternal in a transfigured and glorified form, even if it may be wholly incomprehensible to us at present. It still brings Him very near to us as we remember that He carried His humanity back with Him to heaven (Hebrews 2:14–18).

"He led captivity captive" (Ephesians 4:8 KJV). His ascension was His triumphant return to heaven and indicated that the tyrannical reign of sin was ended and His reign was underway.

R. H. Laver writes:

The ascension helped to clarify the nature of the role of the Messiah to the apostles. They expected a Davidic king, whereas the crucifixion presented them with a suffering Servant. Then the resurrection proclaimed a king after all. The ascension further clarified the nature of His Kingship. The Kingdom of Christ is indeed not of this world. He will reign, but it shall not be simply from an earthly throne. His Kingdom will be glorious but it shall not be achieved through the blood and steel of men. The Cross was the decisive and atoning conflict; the resurrection was the proclamation of triumph; the ascension was the Conqueror's return with the captives of war which issued in the enthronement of the victorious King. *(31 Days)*

A Vision of God and Oneself

The vision of God inevitably results in a vision of oneself and a sense of unworthiness and impurity. The beatific vision deflated Moses. It caused Daniel to see the corruption, not of his vices only but of what he had considered his virtues. It blinded Saul. It threw John on his face before the angel. It punctured Isaiah's complacency.

We all instinctively shrink from the embarrassment of this personal vision. We tend to react adversely to preachers whose message has a subjective edge to it pointing at us, because it seems to downgrade our self-esteem. We much prefer an objective message that does not expose us to our true selves. But God is not so lenient. If we allow Him, He will ruthlessly strip away all camouflage concealing our sins, both conscious and unconscious, and reveal us to ourselves as He sees us.

In light of this, there was the collapse of Isaiah's complacency: "Woe is me for I am ruined!" Isaiah was no lukewarm prophet. Indeed, judged by human standards he was probably the most upright man in the nation. Like Paul, in the sight of the Law he would be blameless. But when he came into the dazzling whiteness of God's holiness, all he could do was to utter the cry of the leper:

"Unclean, unclean!" He saw that God was eternally opposed to all that was evil, even in those who claimed an intimate relationship with Him.

The contemporary philosophy is to say that our greatest need is more self-reliance and self-confidence. If we are to judge by Isaiah's experience, God indicates that our greatest need is self-abasement and a deep sense of insufficiency that will cast us back on Him. *(BF)*

Ignorance and Forgiveness

esus said, "Father, forgive them, for they do not know what they are doing" (Luke 23:34). It seems as though He was trying to find some extenuating circumstance that might lessen their guilt. His sense of justice was not held back by His agony, and He assigned degrees of guilt. This plea limits His "forgive them," so that Judas and Pilate and some of the religious leaders are excluded from the benefits of His intercession. Unlike the majority, they had not acted in ignorance. Judas and Pilate knew what they were doing. They had both weighed Jesus' claims and had acted deliberately. But to the minds of many of the Jews, blinded by hatred, Jesus was no more than a blasphemous impostor. He therefore cried out that their action was due to ignorance not of the *fact* of their crime but of its *enormity.*

In keeping with our Lord's plea, Peter later said to his own kinsmen, "I know that you acted in ignorance, as did your leaders" (Acts 3:17). Paul too conceded that if "they had [understood it], they would not have crucified the Lord of glory" (1 Corinthians 2:8). But their ignorance did not excuse their guilt, or Christ would not have needed to pray, "Forgive them." Even those who did not know what they were doing needed forgiveness. Ignorance may lessen the criminal aspects of sin, but it never exonerates the sin. Their ignorance did not make their sin excusable, but it meant that they themselves were forgivable.

"We must beware of supposing," wrote Bishop J. C. Ryle, "that ignorance is not blameworthy, and that ignorant persons deserve to be forgiven for their sins. At this rate ignorance would be a desirable thing. All spiritual ignorance is more or less culpable. It is part of man's sin that he does not know better than he does. On the other hand we cannot fail to observe in Scripture that sins of ignorance are less sinful before God than sins of knowledge, and that no case is so apparently hopeless as that of the man who sins willfully against the light." *(31 Days)*

The Art of Prayer

"When I go to prayer," confessed an imminent Christian, "I find my heart so loath to go to God, and when it is with Him, so loath to stay." Self-discipline has a key role. "When you feel most indisposed to pray, do not yield to it," he counseled, "but strive to pray, even when you think you cannot."

Mastering the art of prayer, like anything else, takes time. The time we give it will be a true measure of its importance to us. We always find the time for important things. The most common excuse for little time spent in prayer is the list of "to do's" that crowd our day—all our many duties. To Martin Luther, an extra load of duties was reason enough to pray more, not less. Here are his plans for the next day's work: "Work, work from early till late. In fact I have so much to do that I shall spend the first three hours in prayer."

If Luther was both busy and prayed, so can we. Try to explain exactly how prayer works, and you will quickly run into some very difficult explanations. But people who are skeptical of prayer's validity and power are usually those who do not practice it seriously or fail to obey when God reveals His will. We cannot learn about prayer except

239

by praying. No theory has ever enabled a soul to pray. The intellectual problems associated with prayer are solved in the joy of answered prayer and closer fellowship with God.

The Christian leader who seeks an example to follow does well to turn to the life of Jesus Himself. Our belief in the necessity of prayer comes from observing His life. Surely if anyone could have sustained life without prayer, it would be the very Son of God Himself. If prayer were trite or unnecessary, Jesus would not have wasted His time at it. But prayer was the dominant feature of His life and a recurring part of His teaching. Prayer kept His vision of His Father's will sharp and clear. Prayer gave Him courage to endure the perfect but painful will of His Father. Prayer paved the way for transfiguration. To Jesus, prayer was not a hasty add-on, but a joyous necessity. *(BB)*

Genuine Humility

Perhaps John the Baptist's most distinctive quality was his genuine humility, distinctive because it was so rare. Test him at any point and he rang true. Never once did he turn his immense popularity to his own advantage. He was humble in his claims and consistently self-effacing. His amazing ministry demanded an explanation, but when asked if he was the Messiah, he immediately rejected the idea.

"Elijah?"

"No."

"That prophet?" (Deuteronomy 18:15; John 1:21, 25).

"No."

"Then who are you?" the people demanded.

"Oh, I am only a nameless voice. I am not the bridegroom. I am simply His friend." Instead of capitalizing on this opportunity of gaining notoriety, he delighted in anonymity.

John's testimony was never egocentric, always christocentric. He was presented with a unique opportunity for self-glorification when his listeners wondered if John might be the Christ. Instead of launching on a glowing autobiography, he proceeded to proclaim the greatness of his coming Lord. Little wonder that Jesus spoke highly of John, saying he was the Elijah to come. John spoke of Christ's power: "one mightier than I"; His precedence: "He was before me"; His preeminence: "He . . . is above all" (John 3:31 KJV).

John's joy reached its peak when everyone forgot him as they listened to the Bridegroom's voice: "The friend of the bridegroom . . . rejoiceth greatly because of the bridegroom's voice: this my joy therefore is fulfilled" (John 3:29 KJV). He rejoiced when his disciples left him to follow Jesus (John 1:37). Not every preacher is willing to alienate his own congregation in favor of the preacher around the corner! He was gratified even when Jesus' fame grew at the cost of his own: "He must increase, but I must decrease" (John 3:30 KJV). The glory of the Messiah meant more to him than his own glory. These are surely the hallmarks of true humility. *(BF)*

Fear Him Who Destroys

ur Lord affirmed that the fundamental purpose of His coming was "to seek and to save that which was lost" (Luke 19:10 KJV). What is the meaning of that term as He used it? Its serious implications are seen in the fact that it is the same word as "perish" in John 3:16 and "destroy" in Matthew 10:28 (KJV). "Fear him which is able to destroy both soul and body in hell." The idea behind this is not "abolition of existence" but "waste" and "ruin."

In the threefold parable of Luke 15, Jesus used the illustration of the lost coin, the lost sheep, and the lost son. The coin was carelessly lost; the sheep was heedlessly lost; the son was willfully lost. But each was still lost and required to be found by someone else (vv. 4, 8, 32). Being lost is the antithesis of the blessedness implied in the word *saved* in its widest meaning. It is a term that describes not only a present condition and a sinful character but also a coming disaster in which all unregenerate people are involved. "The Lord Jesus shall be revealed from heaven with his mighty angels, in flaming fire taking vengeance on them that know not God, and that obey not the gospel of our Lord Jesus Christ: who shall be punished with everlasting destruction from the presence of the Lord, and from the glory of his power" (2 Thessalonians 1:7–9 KJV). In His atoning death Christ had in view, not merely the improvement of people's personal and social conditions, but their salvation from both a sinful state and an awful destiny.

It should be noted that it is not those who hear of Christ and reject Him, as distinct from those who have never had a chance, who are lost. Jesus came to save those who were *already* lost, who were "condemned already" (John 3:18 KJV). Paul wrote, "If our gospel be hid, it is hid to them that are lost" (2 Corinthians 4:3 KJV)—not merely in danger of being lost but already lost in their separation from God. People do not need to wait until they die to perish. Death will only make visible in the final state of life what is already a fact in this life. *(HL)*

Instruction for Converts

*M*any promising converts have made little progress in the new life of the Spirit simply because they were not correctly instructed at the time of their conversion. It is not wise to overload newborn babes with sage advice, but several things should be made crystal clear to them.

- To be happy, Christians must confess Christ to others at the earliest possible moment, preferably to their own family and circle of friends first and then to their workmates (Romans 10:9, 10). They must be out to experience God's best for their life. Would-be secret disciples never know the real joy of the Lord. Explain that if they trust their newly found Savior, He will give them the power to testify on His behalf (Philippians 4:13).

- Show them that Christ is not only their Savior but their Lord (Romans 10:9 ASV) and that therefore their will must be fully surrendered to their Master.

- Urge them to read the Bible every day first thing in the morning if possible, and ask the Holy Spirit to make the Bible come alive to them. Explain that the Bible is to the spiritual life what bread is to the physical life and that they cannot grow spiritually without "food."

- Having heard God's voice in the Bible, new converts should be instructed to let God hear their voice in prayer, to pour out their soul and their desires before God (Matthew 6:6). Make clear that it is their privilege to talk with God and walk with God every hour of the day and to claim the fulfillment of His promises. Encourage the habit of spontaneous prayer throughout the day as well as quality time spent in solitude with God.

- Advise them to begin to work diligently for Christ and seek to win others to Him. *(DA)*

Interceding for the Lost

The worker whose supreme desire and passion is to be used in cooperation with the Holy Spirit in the winning of converts to Christ must master in some degree the holy art of intercession. If the Master wept and prayed over lost souls, then His servant must do the same. Prayer must always occupy a preeminent place in an evangelism program, for the salvation of the soul is not a human but a divine work. Only through prayer can the power of God be released.

If prayer, then, occupies so important a place, it follows that whatever hinders us in its exercise must be sacrificed. Any price is worth paying that will make us more powerful in prayer. If God is to answer our prayers, we must be sure that we are standing on praying ground. The psalmist warns: "If I regard [cling to] iniquity in my heart, the Lord will not hear me" (Psalm 66:18 KJV), let alone answer me. Before we are on true holy ground, we must have renounced every sin about which the Holy Spirit has convicted us. Have you done this, or is there a barrier between your soul and God? You will know when the last thing has been dealt with.

247

Then it is necessary that we have a heart separated from itself and its own concerns, a heart that is able to bear the burden of lost souls and to intercede for them in the birth process until the new life is implanted. Listen to the apostle Paul as he prays, and note how his prayers are all for others. "I could wish that myself were accursed from Christ for my brethren, my kinsmen according to the flesh" (Romans 9:3 KJV). Mark Epaphras, "always labouring fervently . . . in prayers" (Colossians 4:12 KJV). *(DA)*

The Meaning of Meekness

he word *meek* is more than an unassuming personality or mere mild disposition. Its meaning has been distorted by the line in the children's hymn "Gentle Jesus, meek and mild." He was meek but was far from mild. The impression the hymn leaves is that Jesus was rather weak and ineffective. In fact, He was the very opposite of weak.

Was it mildness He displayed when, alone and with an uplifted whip, He drove the materialistic traffickers with their sheep and cattle out of the temple? He was anything but servile and spineless. When He asked the disciples who men said that He was, they replied, "Some say Elijah, some John the Baptist"—two of the most rugged characters in the Bible! The word *meek* was used of a horse that had been broken and domesticated, giving the idea of energy and power, controlled and directed.

In heaven, the seven angels sing the Song of Moses and the Lamb (Revelation 15:3)—Moses, the meekest man on earth, and Jesus, who said, "I am meek and lowly in heart." But both could blaze with sinless anger when the interests of God were at stake. Meekness is no spineless quality.

This virtue challenges the world's standards. "Stand up for your rights!" is the strident cry of our day. "The world is yours if you can get it." Jesus said, on the contrary, that the world is yours if you renounce it. The meek, not the aggressive, inherit the earth. The meek have an inheritance. The worldly have no future. "They will inherit the earth."

"Blessed are those who hunger and thirst for righteousness, for they will be filled" (Matthew 5:6) or "O the bliss of the unsatisfied."

The blessing promised here is not for mere wistfulness or lukewarm desire for God. It is for those who have a passionate craving not after happiness alone but after righteousness—a right relationship with God. The truly blessed person is the one who hungers and thirsts after God Himself, not only the blessings He gives. David knew that aspiration when he wrote, "As the deer pants for streams of water, so my soul pants for you, O God" (Psalm 42:1). *(SD)*

God Carries on the Work

God is surely eager to use the powers of gifted people, but few of them are as willing as Paul was to place those gifts without reservation at God's disposal. When such people learn to rely not on their own power and wisdom but to depend on God, there is no limit to their usefulness in God's service.

Toward the end of his life, A. B. Simpson was at a great convention when a respected New York minister observed that there was no one similarly qualified to continue leadership of the organization when Simpson's tenure was done. The minister suggested that a large endowment be established to ensure that the work continued. Simpson said and did nothing in response. He believed that if his work was from God, nothing could dismantle it; if it were not from God, no good purpose was served by keeping it going.

Simpson rejoiced during the last months of his life when he had retired from leadership in the Alliance as reports came in of increased missionary offerings and progress on the foreign fields. The year after his death proved to be the most prosperous year in the history of the society.

No greater tribute could be paid to the quality of Simpson's leadership.

Only one Leader holds office forever; no successor is needed for Him. The disciples made no move to appoint a replacement for Jesus, clear evidence that they were conscious of the abiding presence of their living leader and Lord. At times the church has lost a vivid sense of Jesus' presence, but there has never been the panic cry of a leaderless army. The perils and distress of the church weigh deeply on Jesus' heart.

"We tell our Lord plainly," said Martin Luther, "that if He will have His Church then He must look to and maintain and defend it, for we can neither uphold nor protect it; and if we could, then we should become the proudest donkeys under heaven."

Since our Leader conducts His work in the power of an endless life—He is the same yesterday, today, and forever—changes in human leadership should not shake or dismay us. *(SL)*

Proclaiming the Kingdom

In His reply, "Let the dead bury their own dead, but you go and proclaim the kingdom of God" (Luke 9:60), Jesus implied that if this would-be disciple were to put God's interests first, his family interests would not suffer. In any case, even if a literal funeral were involved, there would doubtless be other relatives who did not share his discipleship and were not concerned about the interests of the kingdom who would attend to the funeral arrangements. All other interests must come second for those who desire to be true disciples. They must learn—and so must we—that where there is a clash of interests, Christ can be divisive.

God is not indifferent to family relationships and responsibilities. He does not speak with two voices, urging great care and compassion in those relations on the one hand and then making harsh, contrary demands on the other. But even home ties must come second to His requirements. In setting out the conditions of discipleship in Luke 14, Jesus further clarified the issue: "If anyone comes to me and does not hate his father and mother, his wife and children, his brothers and sisters—yes, even his own life—he cannot be my disciple" (v. 26). When Christ is given unrivaled love and obedience, Jesus promised wonderful rewards, and no one would be the loser in the long run, even amidst earthly sacrifice.

This can be much more than an academic problem in Christian service, especially in the realm of missions. The call of God comes to some disciples to leave home and preach the kingdom overseas. What of aged parents and other relatives left behind?

Where there is an absolute need and there are no other acceptable alternatives, the right course would be for the candidate to stay at home until the situation changes. Otherwise, despite the pull of natural affection, the course for the committed disciple is clear. "Go and proclaim the kingdom of God" (9:60). Unsympathetic or unspiritual relatives and friends may be critical, but our primary loyalty is to our Lord and Master. *(SD)*

Lordship Salvation

In recent times in evangelical circles a strident debate has developed around what has been termed *lordship salvation,* a name that has been applied to the view that, for salvation, a person must believe in Christ as Savior and submit to His authority as Lord. Some, at the other end of the spectrum, go so far as to say that to invite an unsaved person to receive Jesus Christ as Savior and Lord is a perversion of the gospel and is adding to the scriptural teaching about salvation. "All that is required for salvation is believing the gospel message," says Thomas L. Constable.

On both sides are godly people whose love for the Lord is beyond question, and each view aims to preserve the purity of the gospel presentation in our day. There must, therefore, be mutual respect, but both positions cannot be right.

In my view, it is defective teaching to divorce the saving aspects of Christ's work from His lordship. Your acquiring salvation consists of not merely believing certain doctrinal facts; it includes trusting in and embracing the divine Person who is Lord of the universe and who atoned for our sins.

To suggest that people can exercise saving faith in Christ while knowingly rejecting His right to lordship over their life seems a ludicrous suggestion. In salvation we are not accepting Christ in His separate offices. To deliberately say, "I will receive Him as Savior, but I will leave the matter of lordship until later and then decide whether or not I will bow to His will," puts one in an impossible position and cannot be sustained by Scripture.

Having said that, I would concede that many have genuinely believed in Christ who, through inadequate teaching, were never confronted with Christ's claim to lordship, and therefore they have not knowingly rejected it. The proof of the reality of their regeneration would be that as soon as they learn of Christ's claim, they submit to His mastery.

Christ's call was not merely to believe in Him but to be His disciple, and that involves more than "making a decision" or believing certain doctrinal facts. A disciple is one who learns of Christ with the purpose of obeying what he or she learns. Jesus did not commission His disciples to go and make *believers* of all nations, but *disciples;* the terms are not synonymous, although there can be no salvation without believing (Matthew 28:20). *(SD)*

Imperfect Leaders

*S*pirituality does not guarantee infallible judgment. Spirit-filled people are less likely to make mistakes of judgment than their secular counterparts, but perfection eludes us all, whatever our level of spiritual development. Even the apostles made mistakes that required divine correction.

Spiritual leaders who have given such a significant share of their lives to knowing God, to prayer, and to wrestling with the problems of renewal and revival may find it difficult to concede the possibility of misjudgment or mistake. Surely leaders must be people of strength and decisiveness, to stand for what they believe. But willingness to concede error and to defer to the judgment of one's peers increases one's influence rather than diminishes it. Followers will lose confidence in leaders who appear to believe they are infallible. It is strange but true that a perception of infallibility in one area of life often coexists with great humility in other areas.

Many influential Christians have fallen before the temptation of indispensability. It seems that Christians are especially prone to it. They cling to authority long after it should have passed to younger people. I met a wonderful Christian in his nineties who was still superintendent of his church's Sunday school. Younger people were willing and available, but no one in the church had been able to approach this saint about retirement. One unfortunate consequence is that young people who have energy to fill a role are held up and stagnate.

Sometimes sincere and well-meaning followers encourage the notion of indispensability, which feeds a leader's ego and makes him or her even less objective about performance in office. And we can become less objective about our work as we get older.

Missionaries who have raised a church to believe that they are indispensable have done the church an injustice. From the earliest days of the work, missionaries should be planning on working their way out of a job. National leadership needs to learn how to depend on the Lord, how to train its own spiritual leaders, and how to take responsibility for the work. *(SL)*

Sharing God's Glory

There are three groups of people who in Scripture are said to share the glory of the enthroned Christ.

The first group includes those who had remained loyal to Christ amid the trials of this earthly life. Their service had not been perfect, but they had remained true despite opposition. "You are those who have stood by me in my trials. And I confer on you a kingdom, just as my Father conferred one on me, so that you may eat and drink at my table in my kingdom and sit on thrones, judging the twelve tribes of Israel" (Luke 22:28–30).

As recognition of their loyalty, they are accorded seats of honor at the heavenly banquet, sitting at His table. If we display a similar loyalty, we shall doubtless receive the same reward.

They will also "sit on thrones, judging the twelve tribes of Israel" (v. 30). In those days, as today, the king as supreme judge of the high court had legal assessors who sat with him, and no doubt this was the figure the Lord had in mind.

The second class of believers who reign with the Lord certainly includes the martyrs for Christ and may possibly include all believers. "Do you not know that the saints will judge the world? And if you are to judge the world, are you not competent to judge trivial cases?" (1 Corinthians 6:2). "I saw thrones on which were seated those who had been given authority to judge. And I saw the souls of those who had been beheaded because of their testimony for Jesus and because of the word of God" (Revelation 20:4).

The third group includes those who are the overcomers among the churches. "To him who overcomes, I will give the right to sit with me on my throne, just as I overcame and sat down with my Father on his throne" (Revelation 3:21). "To him who overcomes and does my will to the end, I will give authority over the nations" (Revelation 2:26). *(HB)*

The Senior Partner

Some businesses operate quite successfully with one member being a working partner and the other being a silent partner. The latter, though not involved in the day-to-day conduct of the business, makes an essential contribution by providing the capital for the operation. He or she, of course, shares proportionately in the profits.

The Holy Spirit, however, will not consent to be a silent partner, although He may be a secret partner in the sense that He is not visible in the partnership business. He must be given the role of senior partner and have control of the whole enterprise if there is to be a harmonious and successful operation.

Could not many of our failures be attributed to the fact that we give to ourselves the role of senior partner instead of surrendering it to Him? Have we been guilty of trying to make use of Him instead of allowing Him to make use of us?

The story of Gideon illustrates this point. He became a powerful instrument in God's hands because he recognized correctly the relative positions of the Holy Spirit and himself: "Then the Spirit of the LORD came upon [clothed himself with] Gideon" (Judges 6:34).

261

Gideon's personality voluntarily became a garment, so to speak, in which God could move among people. He was thus enabled, through Gideon, to achieve a notable victory on behalf of His people.

When Dwight L. Moody and his wife were vacationing beside the Syrian Sea, an old man greatly amazed Moody by saying, "Young man, honor the Holy Spirit or you shall break down."

"I was angry," Moody said, "but he was right. I was troubled, and prayed until there came a night when the Third Heaven found me. Since then my soul has known the mystery of Moses' burning bush which burned with fire, but was not consumed."

If in our service we honor the Holy Spirit and consistently respect His position as senior partner, we will not be prone to suffer from the contemporary malady of burnout. We will not be undertaking work for God in our own strength or embarking on enterprises He has not initiated. The last word in any decision must lie with the senior partner. *(SD)*

Paul's Great Ambition

Paul was a passionately ambitious man, even before his conversion. He could do nothing by halves. "I was exceedingly zealous," he declared. Always impatient of the confining status quo, he constantly strained toward new goals and horizons. There was a compulsion in him that would brook no denial.

His conversion did not quench the flame of his zeal but rather caused it to leap higher. Whereas his old ambition had been to efface the name of Jesus and exterminate His church, now he had a passion to exalt the name of Jesus and establish and edify His church. His new ambition found its center in the glory of Christ and the advancement of His kingdom.

One writer suggested that Paul suffered from spiritual claustrophobia. His early commission had been to "Go . . . far away to the Gentiles" (Acts 22:21), and he was ambitious to fulfill that commission. He was haunted by the "regions beyond," and every true disciple should share that ambition.

Henry Martyn, brilliant scholar and gallant missionary, expressed his master ambition in these words: "I desire not to burn out for avarice, to burn out for ambition, to burn out for self, but looking up at that great Burnt-offering, to burn out for God and His world."

Paul's ambition was fired by two powerful motives. First was the love of Christ, which "compelled" him and left him no option (2 Corinthians 5:14). That was the love that had captured and broken his rebellious heart. Second was a sense of inescapable obligation. "I feel myself under a sort of universal obligation," he said. "I owe something to all men, from cultured Greek to ignorant savage" (Romans 1:14 PHILLIPS). Since all people were included in the scope of Christ's salvation, he felt equally indebted to all classes. Social status, poverty, and illiteracy were alike irrelevant to him. His ambition was funneled into a single channel—"this one thing I do"—and it unified his whole life. *(SD)*

Extravagant Service

"Why this waste of perfume?"

Why not do something useful with the money it would bring on the market? Why not be practical? You serve God best by serving His creatures. Think of the number of poor people it would have fed! True, it would have fed many, but thank God it was not sold. These men in the house of Simon were thinking practically but not giving Jesus His proper place.

In His ministry Jesus had demonstrated abundantly that He was not indifferent to the plight of the poor. He was constantly ministering to their physical as well as their spiritual needs. It must have hurt this woman deeply when His disciples so harshly rebuked her.

She had some other options open to her: (1) she could have sold the perfume—and turned it into hard cash and done something "useful" with it; (2) she could have saved it as provision for her old age; (3) she could have used it on herself, to enhance her beauty in the Lord's eyes. Are not somewhat similar options open to us in our relationship to the Lord?

"What a waste!" many said when the brilliant young Cambridge scholar Henry Martyn, who at the age of twenty had gained the highest award in mathematics the world had to offer, threw away his prospects for seven years of missionary work. But in those seven years he gave the world the New Testament in three of the major languages of the East.

"What a waste," many said when William Borden, heir to the Borden millions, turned his back on his alluring prospects to become a missionary to the Muslims and died before he reached the field. But that proved to be fruitful waste, for his biography, *Borden of Yale,* has influenced thousands toward the mission field.

Perhaps God is not so economical and utilitarian as we are. What waste and "lavish spending" we see in His creation! But there are some things of the heart and the spirit that cannot be measured in cold cash.

How much do we know in practice of this seemingly wasteful and extravagant expenditure of ourselves in His service out of simple love for Him? Or are we stingy and calculating in our self-giving? "Whoever sows sparingly will also reap sparingly" (2 Corinthians 9:6). *(SD)*

A Strong Devotional Life

J A M E S   4 : 8

In the culture of the soul, no habit is more crucial and formative than maintaining a consistent devotional life—a regular time reserved for fellowship and communion with God. Not everyone finds that easy, but its importance and value cannot be exaggerated. Since that is the case, it is only reasonable to expect that the habit will be the focus of relentless attack from our adversary.

Although it may not always be possible, there is both logical and spiritual value in observing the first hour of the day.

Later hours of the day have routine duties that must be performed. Interruptions often break the routine, but in spite of these, it is most helpful to establish a regular routine that enables you to breathe the incense of heaven before inhaling the smog and fog of earth.

In the earlier quiet hour the mind can be adjusted before meeting people or facing difficult problems. The day's duties and responsibilities can be committed to God. We can memorize a Scripture verse to chew on during the day. We should be alert to look for some special thought or message in our reading.

We can relate the principles of Scripture to the details of daily life, remembering that the Bible contains principles to guide, commands to obey, warnings to heed, examples to emulate, and promises to claim.

With regard to prayer in our quiet time, we should first seek to realize the presence of God. He encouraged us with the words, "Draw near to God and He will draw near to you" (James 4:8 NASB). Communion with another has two sides, so silence is sometimes appropriate in efforts to hear the voice of God.

Pray audibly if that helps in concentration. If privacy is difficult to find, retreat into the inner part of your soul. In the evening, review the day with confession and thanksgiving, and let your last thoughts be of God. *(SD)*

Unanswered Prayer

Our Lord's brother gives one reason for unanswered prayer: "When you ask, you do not receive, because you ask with wrong motives" (James 4:3). God does not attempt to answer every self-centered petition, but He does promise to answer every prayer that is according to His good and perfect will.

It may be that our prayer was not the prayer of faith but only the prayer of hope. Jesus said, "According to your faith will it be done to you" (Matthew 9:29), not according to your hope. Are many of your prayers only prayers of hope?

Or we may have been substituting faith in prayer for faith in God. We are not told anywhere to have faith in prayer but to "have faith in God," the One who answers the prayer. This is more than a matter of semantics. Sometimes we sigh, "Our prayers are so weak and ineffective!" or "My faith is so small!" Jesus anticipated this reaction when He said, "I tell you the truth, if you have faith as small as a mustard seed, you can say to this mountain, 'Move from here to there' and it will move. Nothing will be impossible for you" (Matthew 17:20).

The naked eye sees little difference between a grain of sand and a mustard seed, but there is a world of difference between the two. In the mustard seed is the germ of life. It is not the size of our faith that is important, but whether it is a living faith in a living God.

Mature disciples will not become discouraged because of a delay in the answer to their prayer. They know that a delayed answer is not necessarily a denied answer.

God's timing is infallible. He takes every factor and contingency into account. We often want to pluck unripe fruit, but He will not be pressured into premature action.

If He in His wisdom delays the answer to our prayer, that delay will in the long run prove to be for our good. (See Hebrews 12:10.) It will be either because He has some better thing for us or because there is something He desires to achieve in our lives that can come about in no other way. *(SD)*

Money: A Test of Character

f we have sown spiritual seed among you, is it too much if we reap a material harvest from you? If others have this right of support from you, shouldn't we have it all the more? But we did not use this right" (1 Corinthians 9:11–12).

In support of his contention, the apostle cites the generally accepted principle that the farmer who produces the crop has the right to a share of it, as also the grower of grapes a share of the wine. In other words, there is nothing wrong in being a paid preacher. Even the ox is not muzzled (kept from eating) when he is engaged in threshing the grain. "In the same way, the Lord has commanded that those who preach the gospel should receive their living from the gospel" (v. 14).

Throughout his ministry Paul was meticulous in his financial dealings. He refused to allow monetary considerations to influence his decisions or actions. Money is an acid test of character. Our real riches are the quality of our character, and these remain with us eternally. In his attitude toward money, Paul was pure—something that cannot be said of all Christian workers. He had victory in the realm of finance, and he renounced his right to be supported by the church so that he might win more souls to Christ (v. 12).

Whether we possess much money or little, our attitude toward it is revealing. There is no moral quality in riches or poverty per se, but our attitude toward it is a test of true spirituality. In a world in which material and financial values are paramount, it is not easy to escape their corruption.

Discover a person's attitude toward money, and you will learn a great deal about his or her character. Not every Christian worker has mastered the problem of financial stewardship, and, as a result, many have lost spiritual effectiveness. Paul did not fall into that trap. *(SD)*

The Living One

"I am he that liveth, and was dead" (Revelation 1:18 KJV), expressing the vivid contrast between the eternal life inherent in Christ and His voluntary surrender to the powers of death. Because He tasted death, He is able to say to death-ridden humanity, "There is no need to fear death. I have trodden that way, exhausted its power, and extracted its sting."

"I am alive for evermore" (v. 18 KJV), for all the ages. Death could not keep its prey. He now lives in "the power of an endless life" (Hebrews 7:16 KJV). Others, like Lazarus, had returned to life only to die again. Christ rose from the dead and is alive forevermore. His having passed through death as a man and now living in fullness of life is the basis for our confidence, since through Him death is but the gateway to fuller life. To a church facing the possibility of martyrdom, this truth was urgently needed to quell their fear. The church could not live if Christ were dead, but because Christ lives, the church cannot die.

In saying, "[I] have the keys of hell and of death" (v. 18 KJV), Christ wrested death in His resurrection from "him that hath the power of death, the devil" (Hebrews 2:14 KJV). Hades is portrayed in Matthew 16:18 as a prison

273

house or walled city. It is the unseen world to which death is the portal. Keys are the symbol of authority. The keys of the unseen world are in Christ's hand and with them the destiny of all people. We need have no fear of going to any place when the keys are in His nail-pierced hand. No longer need we fear the figure of the grim reaper, the king of terrors. Christ alone admits us to death and opens the way out on the other side. No one can wrest the keys from His control. Because He rose, we shall rise also.

Because this living, majestic, powerful Christ stands in the midst of His churches and holds their destiny in these hands, there is no cause for them or for us to fear. *(SM)*

Never Alone

In writing of the single state in 1 Corinthians 7, Paul three times says concerning singleness, "It is good." His whole emphasis is that the single lifestyle is honorable and good; but not all singles share Paul's opinion. There is something to be said, however, for the view that with so many marriages ending in divorce and so many battered wives, "single bliss is better than marital misery." It should not be forgotten that a large part of the missionary enterprise is carried on by single women.

Divorce is essentially and inevitably a lonely experience for those who are involved. The pain is not over when the decree is signed; indeed, it has just begun. The world is full of lonely divorced people. One tragic side effect is that the children lose one parent—sometimes two. Inevitably that creates loneliness for the innocent victims of divorce.

The lot of the widow or widower is not enviable. Even when the marriage had not been ideal, there was at least some companionship, and there was fellowship at meals. In the early days of bereavement due to divorce, there is usually a great deal of support from friends and loved ones, but then life simply goes on for them. Visits and

275

invitations inevitably grow fewer. In many cases the widower is more poorly equipped to handle the changed situation than is the widow.

Bereavement is a desolating experience, and in the earlier stages one feels that the sun will never shine again. It should be accepted that it is not wrong or weak to grieve. Grief should be unashamedly expressed. Tears are therapeutic. Bereavement must be accepted as part of the human situation.

Although time does not remove the sense of loss, it does blunt the sharp edge of the sorrow. But immeasurably more potent than time is the comfort of God. "Praise be to . . . the God of all comfort, who comforts us in all our troubles, so that we can comfort those in any trouble with the comfort we ourselves have received from God" (2 Corinthians 1:3–4).

Some people hang on to their sorrow and, like the psalmist, refuse to be comforted, thus cheating themselves of the very thing they most need—the comfort of God. Jesus appropriated Isaiah 61:1 to Himself: "He has sent me to bind up the brokenhearted." Let Him do it, whether it be a divorce or some other tragedy in your life. *(SD)*

The Potter and the Clay

The patriot-prophet Jeremiah was heartbroken. Despite his tears and entreaties, his beloved nation had proven stubborn and was drifting further and further from God. His earnest endeavors to avert catastrophe had proved fruitless. He had exhausted all his own resources, and there seemed no alternative to deserved judgment.

It was just when he had reached this crisis that God gave Jeremiah a vision of hope. "Go down to the potter's house" the Lord said, "and there I will give you my message" (Jeremiah 18:2). Although Israel had persistently thwarted the divine purpose of blessing, if the nation would repent and once again yield to His touch, the heavenly Potter would make it into a new nation and give it another chance, even at this late hour.

Although the vision was a contemporary message to Israel, the application is timeless. Just as the elements of the potter's art are essentially the same as in Jeremiah's day, so are God's methods and dealings with His children in every age. The context and trappings may differ, but the underlying principles are unchanging.

When Jeremiah went obediently to the potter's house, he saw the revolving wheel controlled by the potter's foot;

a pile of clay inert and unable to improve its condition, of no intrinsic value; a pot of water for use in softening the clay and making it moldable; a scrap heap on which the potter cast the pots that had failed to realize his design; and, of course, he saw the skillful and experienced potter himself. "Then the word of the LORD came to me," Jeremiah wrote. " 'O house of Israel, can I not do with you as this potter does?' declares the LORD. 'Like clay in the hand of the potter, so are you in my hand'" (vv. 5–6).

That assertion of the absolute, sovereign power of God sounds rather harsh and forbidding. His power is so final, and we are so powerless. But Isaiah the prophet softens the picture: "O LORD, you are our Father. We are the clay, you are the potter; we are all the work of your hand" (Isaiah 64:8).

True, God is sovereign in His power, but He also has a father's heart. We can be absolutely certain that His sovereignty will never clash with His paternity. All His dealings with His frail and failing children are dictated by unchanging love. *(SD)*

Signs of Christ's Return

To a unique degree this generation has witnessed the universal and dramatic fulfillment of prophecy. Many of the signs Jesus said would herald His return have developed before our eyes.

The Evangelistic Sign. "This gospel of the kingdom will be preached in the whole world as a testimony to all nations, and then the end will come" (Matthew 24:14).

This prophecy has been fulfilled in our generation to a degree that has never before been the case. There is now no major nation in which there is no Christian witness. But as Christ has not yet returned, it is obvious that our task has not been fully completed.

The Religious Sign. "That day will not come until the rebellion occurs and the man of lawlessness is revealed" (2 Thessalonians 2:3).

Unfortunately, we can see this sign being fulfilled all around us. As Jesus foretold, the love of many is growing cold (Matthew 24:12). But also in many parts of the world there is an unprecedented gathering of the harvest, so we do not need to be discouraged.

The Political Sign. Could prevailing world conditions have been more accurately and comprehensively described

279

than in our Lord's words in Luke 21:25–26? "There will be signs . . . On the earth, nations will be in anguish and perplexity . . . Men will faint from terror, apprehensive of what is coming on the world."

The Jewish Sign. "Jerusalem will be trampled on by the Gentiles until the times of the Gentiles are fulfilled" (Luke 21:24).

There are broad and general signs that Jesus gave to His disciples as precursors of His return. These and many other signs have been intensified and have come to fulfillment in our day. For the first time in 2,500 years, Jerusalem is not dominated by Gentiles.

Whatever view we hold regarding the details surrounding the second coming of Christ, if we fail to discern in these broad signs an intimation of the imminence of His return, we should deserve a similar rebuke. History is moving rapidly—not to cataclysm merely, but to consummation. *(SD)*

Learning New Skills

The adage "an old dog cannot be taught new tricks" is one of the myths associated with old age that should be exposed and discarded. It may take longer to acquire new skills—but we need to overcome fear of both failure and lack of ability. Research at the Duke University Center for the Study of the Aging showed "the slowing down" process can be caused by unconscious anxiety. When the subjects took drugs that counteracted anxiety, improved performance resulted.

The elderly can do many things. New learning skills can be acquired quite late in life. Fear that one is too old, rather than a lack of brainpower, prevents people from making the attempt. "New tricks" take longer to learn because the brain and nervous system tend to slow down.

Toward the end of her life, my wife was suffering from multiple sclerosis. The trouble first appeared in her hands, and gradually she lost the use of thumb and first finger. Before this time she had never attempted painting, but with encouragement, she took it up and found she had quite an unusual gift. When she lost the use of her thumb and finger, she used the remaining ones. Her work was of such quality that she was admitted as a member of the

281

Fellowship of Artists. When she became so limited that she could do little else, she was still able to paint. During the two years of her illness, she completed forty or fifty paintings that are treasured by relatives and friends. How many other old people may have similar hidden talents that could be uncovered if only they were encouraged to discover it and "give it a go."

As the psychologist Karl Menninger put it, the attitude that it is too late for improving in our old age or that we can't do what we used to do can become an alibi for not doing the things we are capable of learning. To say "What's the good, it's too late" is a prescription for despair. Furthermore, Christians have supernatural aid available to enable them to do all God's will. "I can do all things through Him who strengthens me" (Philippians 4:13 NASB). *(EY)*

Consecrated for Service

P H I L I P P I A N S   2 : 1 2 – 1 3

Is it possible that we may be holding back our lives from the living God because of fear of what it might cost? Dr. Alexander Maclaren said the meaning of being a Christian is that, in response to the gift of a whole Christ, a person gives his or her whole self to Him.

It is a life separated to the glory of God. Inherent in the word *consecration* is the idea of separateness. There must of necessity be separation from sin if there is to be separation to God. "Having therefore these promises . . . let us cleanse ourselves from all filthiness of the flesh and spirit" is Paul's exhortation (2 Corinthians 7:1 KJV). Here again *cleanse* implies a definite, deliberate act. We can renounce everything we know to be wrong by a resolute act of our renewed wills, reinforced by the Holy Spirit (Philippians 2:12–13).

But the separation meant here is not the separation found in the monastery. It is *insulation* from what is sinful rather than *isolation* from it. We have to go on living in a sinful world among sinful people. It is not merely avoiding negative things. Consecrated Christians hate evil, but they have a passion for the right and for the glory of God and Christ. They test all their actions by the one standard: "Is this for the glory of God?" They will do anything, suffer anything, if only God is glorified. Nothing is too costly to give to the Master. Sacrifice has been described as the ecstasy of giving the best we have to the One we love the most.

Then it is a life concentrated on the service of God. Robert Lee tells of a convert who was testifying to the fact that the Lord had helped him along the line of consecration. But he had not gotten the word correctly. He said it two or three times like this: "I'm so glad He helped me to be wholly concentrated unto Him." He may have used the wrong word, but he expressed the right idea.

Consecration will always end in concentration on God and His service. It is not an end in itself. If it does not find expression in holy activity, it is superficial. *(BB)*

The Purpose of Life

2 TIMOTHY 4:6-8

Many people, young and old, are frankly disappointed with life. It has not given them what they have craved, and they are disillusioned and frustrated. The French philosopher Goethe said: "I have been deemed, and I believe justly, one of fortune's favorites. Yet I cannot, as I look back on my life, recall more than three weeks of positive happiness in the whole." This may be rather an extreme case, and yet it is by no means an isolated one. A whole generation of young people could make a similar confession.

By way of contrast, hear Paul's testimony: "I am now ready to be offered, and the time of my departure is at hand. I have fought a good fight, I have finished my course, I have kept the faith: Henceforth there is laid up for me a crown of righteousness, which the Lord, the righteous judge, shall give me at that day" (2 Timothy 4:6–8 KJV). There is no disillusionment or frustration here. He had lived life to the full, had worked hard and suffered much, but at the end he found satisfaction, fulfillment, and reward.

If Paul were challenged and asked what made him what he was and what had enabled him to triumph in such painful and adverse circumstances, he might have replied: "Once I could describe my life like this: For me to live is Paul. But since I saw the vision on the Damascus road, the center of my life has shifted. Now for me to live is Christ." To him life was now someone else.

It is a searching spiritual exercise to examine your life and finish Paul's statement for yourself: "To me to live is _____." There must be some center, some unifying motive to our lives. What is it: self or Christ? Here Paul was saying that since his conversion, the center of life had shifted from him to someone else, and that change had altered the circumference (or circumstances) of his life as well. *(BB)*

Husbands and Wives

"Wives, submit yourselves unto your own husbands, as unto the Lord . . . Therefore as the church is subject unto Christ, so let the wives be to their own husbands in every thing" (Ephesians 5:22–24 KJV). There is no suggestion here that the wife is inferior to the husband in any sense. It is not a question of the superiority of the husband or the inferiority of the wife but of the respective positions God in His wisdom has assigned to each. "The husband is the head of the wife, even as Christ is the head of the church" (v. 23).

As it is no dishonor to the church to be subject to Christ, it is no dishonor for the wife to be subject to her husband. Within the marriage relationship, the wife can wield a tremendous influence, but that influence will be greatly enhanced when her divinely ordained position is recognized.

If we only read this far, the injunction to wives would seem to be sweeping and unfair, but taken in its context and read in conjunction with the equally stringent requirements for husbands, it is not so unreasonable as it may at first seem. If all husbands fulfilled the pattern given in verses 25, 28, and 33, wives would find no problem in being subject to them. The Holy Spirit knew that if wives were in danger of failing in subjection to their husbands, there was an equal danger that husbands would not love their wives unselfishly.

"Husbands, love your wives, even as Christ also loved the church and gave himself for it . . . So ought men to love their wives as their own bodies . . . Let every one of you in particular so love his wife even as himself" (vv. 25, 28, 33 KJV). The unique element in Christ's love for the church is His utter selflessness, His sacrificial love. This quality will be seen in ever-increasing measure in the Spirit-filled husband. Love always expresses itself in generous consideration. The wife has the right to expect from her husband a love that is sacrificial and unselfish. He is to love her as much as he loves himself. *(BB)*

The Sacrifice of Intercession

Both our Lord and Paul made it clear that prayer is no mere idealistic wish fulfillment. "All vital praying makes a drain on a man's vitality," wrote J. H. Jowett. "True intercession is a sacrifice, a bleeding sacrifice." Jesus performed many mighty works without outward sign of strain, but of His praying it is recorded that "he . . . offered up prayers and supplications with strong crying and tears" (Hebrews 5:7 KJV).

Paul told the Colossian Christians that his coworker Epaphras "wrestled" with God in prayer for them. (See Colossians 4:12.) Our lukewarm prayers pale in comparison to Epaphras's intercessions. The word *wrestling* is that from which our word *agony* is derived. It is used of a man toiling at his work until utterly weary (Colossians 1:29) or competing in the arena for the coveted laurel wreath (1 Corinthians 9:25). It describes the soldier "[fighting] the good fight of the faith" (1 Timothy 6:12), or Jesus' servants fighting to prevent His arrest by the Jews, if His kingdom had been of this world (John 18:36). It pictures the agony of a man seeking to save his own soul (Luke 13:24). But its supreme significance appears in the tragedy of Gethsemane. "Being in an agony he prayed more earnestly" (Luke 22:44 KJV), an agony brought on by His identification with and grief over the sins of a lost world. Prayer is a strenuous spiritual exercise that demands the utmost mental discipline and concentration. It may have been because of this fact that our Lord sometimes linked prayer with fasting.

True intercession is costly. Jesus first gave Himself and then made intercession for His murderers. He could do no more for them. Are we asking of God something we ourselves could supply? Can it be true intercession if we don't come to God empty-handed? True intercession demands the sacrifice and dedication of everything; it cannot be either costless or crossless. *(BB)*

Christ's Victory over Satan

Jesus triumphed over Satan in the wilderness and "returned . . . in the power of the Spirit" (Luke 4:1–14). By His death on Calvary, He bound "a strong man fully armed" and took away from him "his armor on which he had relied, and distributes his plunder" (Luke 11:21–22 NASB).

By His vicarious death and victorious resurrection, Christ once and for all answered every charge or accusation that Satan could bring against the child of God. This truth caused Paul to ask his triumphant questions: "Who will bring a charge against God's elect? . . . Who is the one who condemns?" (Romans 8:33–34 NASB). This truth inspired John's ringing declaration: "Now the salvation, and the power, and the kingdom of our God and the authority of His Christ have come, for the accuser of our brethren has been thrown down, who accuses them before our God day and night" (Revelation 12:10 NASB).

Paul further expounds Christ's victory over Satan through the illustration of the exultant march of a victorious Roman general returning after a triumphant campaign. His reward was to march his army through the streets of Rome, leading behind him the captive, weaponless kings and peoples he had conquered. He boldly displayed them as his conquests.

This is the picture in Colossians 2:15. God made a public example and exposed to public disgrace the evil principalities and powers, showing to all that the victory of Calvary had disarmed them and left them impotent. Satan and his hosts have only as much power over the believer as he allows them to have. For did not Christ say, "Behold I have given you authority . . . to overcome *all* the power of the enemy" (Luke 10:19, emphasis added)? Their power over humanity is forever broken. Christ's victory over Satan is our victory over Satan, and it is complete. *(SM)*

The Realm of Satan

It is dangerous for one who is not "in Christ" to intrude into this realm. But Paul's name was feared in hell: "And the evil spirit answered and said to them, 'I recognize Jesus, and I know Paul, but who are you?'" (Acts 19:15 NASB).

There is both comparison and contrast in Satan's working in those who are "sons of the evil one" (Matthew 13:38) and the working of the Holy Spirit in the "children of God." Satan controls and empowers those who pledge allegiance to him. "You formerly walked according to the course of this world, according to the prince of the power of the air, of the spirit that is now working in the sons of disobedience" (Ephesians 2:1–2 NASB). Contrast this with "it is God who is at work in you, both to will and to work for His good pleasure" (Philippians 2:13 NASB). Just as God by the Holy Spirit empowers His messengers, so the devil imparts his satanic deception and strength to his emissaries.

What is the motivation of this host of demons? What inspires them to their hellish and destructive ministry?

First, it is loyalty to their chosen prince, whose kingdom and authority they aim to establish and extend. If all Christ's followers worked as zealously for their King as the demons do for Satan, there would not be two billion unevangelized people in the world! To achieve their objective, the demons carry out unceasing warfare in the interests of their master.

> For our struggle is not against flesh and blood, but against the rulers, against the powers, against the world forces of this darkness, against the spiritual forces of wickedness in the heavenly places (Ephesians 6:12).

Negatively, their motivation springs from an implacable hatred of Christ. Their inflexible purpose is to destroy His church and disrupt His purposes. They know Christ and are aware of His purposes for blessing mankind. Not without a desperate struggle will the determined powers of darkness yield control of a world that lies asleep in the arms of the Evil One. *(SM)*

The Pitfalls of Popularity

What leader or preacher does not desire to be liked by his people? Being disliked is no virtue, but popularity can have too high a price. "Woe unto you, when all men shall speak well of you!" Jesus warned in Luke 6:26 (KJV).

Personality cults have often developed around great spiritual leaders. Followers are awestruck at a leader's virtues and show such fawning deference that the leader seems no longer merely human. Worse yet, the leader sometimes begins to enjoy his or her pedestal.

Paul faced this problem at Corinth. Christians there were splintering into camps promoting their favorite: some liked Apollos, others liked Paul. The apostle saw the danger and immediately put a stop to it. Neither of them deserved such "hero worship," "but only God" (1 Corinthians 3:7). Any fervor, devotion, or loyalty the people in Corinth might have for spiritual leaders should be given solely to the person of Jesus.

Spiritual leaders may be esteemed highly for their work's quality, but that esteem cannot degenerate into a form of idol worship. Leaders must work to draw the people's affection to Jesus. There is no fault in finding encouragement when one's service is appreciated, but the leader must altogether refuse to be idolized.

Stephen Neill said in a lecture to theological students: "Popularity is the most dangerous spiritual state imaginable, since it leads on so easily to the spiritual pride which drowns men in perdition. It is a symptom to be watched with anxiety since so often it has been purchased at the too heavy price of compromise with the world."

George Whitefield was immensely popular, and in his early years he enjoyed the acclaim. He recalled that he felt it was death to be despised and worse than death to be laughed at. But as his service and career progressed, he grew tired of the attention. "I have seen enough of popularity to be sick of it," he declared. *(SL)*

Answers to Temptation

ecause the Christ to whom we are united by faith was victorious over every type of temptation by Satan, we may share in His triumph as we appropriate it by faith.

Here is the essence of the three temptations:

1. The first was the temptation to satisfy a legitimate appetite by illegitimate means.
2. The second was the temptation to produce spiritual results by unspiritual means.
3. The third was the temptation to obtain a lawful heritage by unlawful means.

It is significant that each of Jesus' answers to Satan was a quotation from the book of Deuteronomy. Our Lord thus confirmed the Pentateuch as the Word of God.

Joseph Parker draws attention to some interesting features in our Lord's answers to Satan's suggestions.

- They were not the result of Christ's divine keen intellect that is above and beyond what we sinful humans may claim.

- They were not the outcome of ready wit nor of an unexpected flash of inspiration.
- They do not bear the marks of inventive genius.
- They were not answers that came on the spur of the moment as a result of His infinite wisdom. They were not philosophical arguments elaborately stated and eloquently discussed. *But* they were simple enough for the average child to understand. They were quotations from the Word of God on which He meditated day and night. Only the eternal, all-powerful Word of God will cause Satan to flee defeated. Human reasoning and arguments are weak in conflicts with Satan because they lack authority. *(31 Days)*

Supporting Subordinates

EXODUS 18:18

Once leaders delegate, they should show utmost confidence in the people they have entrusted. A. B. Simpson trusted those in charge of the various schools he founded, leaving them free to exercise their own gifts. If they failed, Simpson took it as a reflection of his own failed leadership, for he had selected them.

Subordinates perform better when they feel sure of the leader's support, whether a given project succeeds or fails, so long as they have acted within the bounds of their assignment. This confidence comes when responsibilities have been clearly defined in writing, to eliminate any misunderstandings. Failing to communicate clearly has led to many unhappy problems.

One of the great biblical illustrations of this principle is the story of Jethro, father-in-law to Moses, recorded in Exodus 18.

Israel emerged from Egypt an unorganized horde of ex-slaves. By the time of Exodus 18, a new national spirit was developing. Jethro saw that Moses faced intolerably heavy burdens—he was dealing with problems from morning till night. Moses was the legislature, the judiciary, and the executive branch of the new nation. His decisions were accepted by the people as God's will.

Jethro saw that Moses could not keep up such a pace and made two solid arguments for delegating some of the work. First, "You and these people who come to you will only wear yourselves out. The work is too heavy for you; you cannot handle it alone" (Exodus 18:18). Moses was probably beyond his limit of physical and emotional resources. Second, the current method of problem-solving was too slow, and people were getting impatient. Sharing authority would speed up legal action, and the people would go away satisfied (18:23).

Then Jethro proposed a two-part plan. Moses would continue to teach spiritual principles and exercise legislative leadership. He would also decide the hard cases at court. But much of his work would be delegated to competent, trustworthy subordinates. Jethro spoke wisely, for if Moses had succumbed under the strain, he would have left chaos behind—no one trained to lead, no one in charge of anything. Failure to make provision for the succession of leadership has spelled ruin for many missions and churches. *(SL)*

He Is Without Sin

The Lord's challenge to His critics still remains unanswered: "Can any of you prove me guilty of sin?" (John 8:46). His sinlessness could not be challenged, or they would have brought a charge against Him. Even hell could bring no accusation. "The prince of this world is coming. He has no hold on me," Jesus claimed (John 14:30).

A study of His life reveals consistent immunity from sin. Never did He show the slightest discontent with His own behavior—which would be a grave sin of pride in any other person. Never did He shed a tear over any failure. He demanded repentance of others yet was never penitent Himself. Nor can this self-satisfaction be explained on the grounds that His standard of duty or sense of moral obligation was less exacting than that of His contemporaries. The reverse was the case. His code of ethics was immeasurably higher than theirs, yet not once does He admit that He has in any degree fallen short of His own exacting standards.

At the end of His life, as Jesus communed with His Father in His moving High Priestly Prayer, He claimed to have accomplished perfectly the work entrusted to Him (John 17:4). In any other case than His, we would be justified in regarding such claims as obnoxious pride and arrogant hypocrisy. In His case the facts substantiated the claim.

To quote T. C. Edwards in this context, "The fact that Jesus never confessed sin implies in His case that He never did sin. In every other good man, the saintlier he becomes the more pitiless is his self-condemnation, and the more severe he is on certain kinds of sin, such as hypocrisy. But Jesus, if He were a sinner, was guilty of the very worst of sin, which He rebuked with burning anger in the Pharisees of His day. Yet He never accuses Himself . . . He never speaks about redeeming Himself but declares Himself to be the paschal lamb 'whose blood of the new covenant is shed for many unto the remission of sins'" (see Matthew 26:28).

While describing the doom of the unrepentant in terrible images, He never mentions His own need for salvation. He prayed, "Father, forgive them," but never, "Father, forgive Me." *(31 Days)*

Nehemiah the Model Leader

Nehemiah's genuine concern for the welfare of others was so obvious that even his enemies noticed it (2:10). He expressed his concern in fasting, prayer, and tears (1:4–6). Nehemiah identified with his people in their sorrows and in their sins: "I confess the sins we Israelites, including myself and my father's house, have committed against you" (v. 6).

Nehemiah exhibited keen foresight. He knew that opposition was sure to arise, so he secured letters from the king for safe passage and for the resources to accomplish the task, "to make beams for the gates of the citadel . . . and for the city wall" (2:8). He carefully planned his strategy.

Through all his adventures and boldness, there runs a strain of caution. He did not jump into the work immediately upon arrival but waited three days to assess the situation (2:11). And when he did get down to business, he did not hold a tell-all press conference but kept his goals largely secret, even doing reconnaissance under cover of night.

Nehemiah could make clear decisions. He did not put off the tough call but cut to the heart and made a judgment. And his decisions were impartial; he did not play favorites. When correction was needed, he gave it to officials and executives as well as to workers (5:7).

Nehemiah was uncommonly empathetic. He listened to grievances and took remedial action (4:10–14; 5:1–13). He let people "weep on his shoulder." He sympathized with others.

Nehemiah was a realist; he understood the mechanics of the real world. "We prayed to our God and posted a guard day and night" (4:9).

He accepted responsibility with the intention of following through on all assignments, the pleasant ones and the dirty ones, until the job was done.

Nehemiah was a vigorous administrator, a calm crisis manager, a fearless initiator, a courageous decision maker, and a persevering leader. He was resolute in the face of threats and vigilant against treachery, a leader who won and held the full confidence of his followers. *(SL)*

The Greatest Teacher

Jesus' favorite formula, "Verily, verily, I say unto thee" (John 3:3), left no room for argument. Those who heard Him teach were amazed at the contrast between Him and the scribes, "because he taught as one who had authority" (Matthew 7:29). Unlike them, He did not have to refer to the teachings of others. His word was authoritative. "Moses said . . . but I say unto you . . ."

It has been well said that His authority was not the charisma of a great reputation but the irresistible force of a divine message delivered with the knowledge of a divine mission.

When Jesus spoke on any subject, nothing more needed to be said. The Jewish leaders could not but recognize this quality, repugnant though it was to them. Even though they were not prepared to recognize His claims to be the Messiah, they were ready to acknowledge His unique gifts as teacher.

No other teacher has so skillfully and successfully combined simplicity and profundity. In His sayings there is an absence of too much scholarship or striving for an effect. None in His audience ever needed to scratch their heads and wonder what the preacher was aiming at, even though they may not have understood the full spiritual significance of the words. "His illustrations are commonplace, His words within the reach of the humblest. Are they real in faith and honest in heart? Then the poorest are capable of recognizing His simple teaching, and following it as in His perfect life," wrote Horace Bushnell.

Our Lord thought in images, and His teaching was full of figures of speech. His parables—concise and pointed stories in figurative style—expressed spiritual truths so vividly that they have affected the lives of all generations. How could He more effectively have portrayed His Father's love than in the parable of the prodigal son? The words of Jesus had an incomparable directness that left a clear and indelible impression on His hearers.

Although Jesus did not contradict the findings of true science or other disciplines in anything He said, He made no overt references to them. Jesus used no technical terms and a minimum of theological expressions in His teaching. Small wonder that "the common people heard him gladly" (Mark 12:37). *(31 Days)*

Humility as a Primary Virtue

The works of the great philosophers of past days do not exalt humility as a virtue. Their lives will be examined in vain for evidence of true Christian humility. The reverse is the case. There is no word in either Greek or Latin that expresses the Christian idea of humility. The word *lowly* (KJV; *humble,* NIV), which Jesus appropriated to Himself, is employed by ethical philosophers such as Socrates, Plato, and Xenophon in a derogatory sense. Even Josephus, the Hebrew historian and moralist, invested the word with a similar meaning. "Humility is a vice with the heathen moralists," said J. B. Lightfoot.

Not until Jesus came with His peerless life and matchless teaching was humility elevated to the level of a primary virtue. Humility as a grace is a foundation stone of Christianity. Since the Greeks used the word generally as signifying someone base or mean-spirited, it is readily understood that our Lord's pronouncements on the subject introduced His disciples to a startlingly new and revolutionary scale of values. "Whoever humbles himself will be exalted" (Matthew 23:12). "He who is least among you all—he is the greatest" (Luke 9:48). It was a difficult lesson for them to master, that humility was to be desired, not despised.

Meekness plus lowliness equals humility. Meekness is humility in relation to God. Lowliness is humility in relation to man. It is possible to be meek and not lowly. Jesus was just as meek toward God as He was lowly before man.

In common usage, meekness is almost synonymous with weakness, or an inferiority complex, and is usually attributed to those who are insignificant. Yet our divine Lord crowned this modest character quality as queen of virtues. Otto Borchert contrasts the genuine humility of the Lord, which manifested itself in the utter absence of any striving after magnification or originality, with Muhammad, who was always sensitive to his personal appearance. The vanity of Buddha peeps through the rags of his beggar's cloak. But Jesus moved about in the unaffected guise of ordinary folk, and they were attracted to Him. "He humbled himself" (Philippians 2:8). *(31 Days)*

Who Is on Trial?

Throughout the crowded closing hours of His life, Jesus said nothing that could in any way be construed as a withdrawal or watering down of the astounding claims to kingship and deity He had made. Although He did not disallow the claim that He was King, He hastened to make clear that His kingdom was not of this world but was a spiritual one (John 18:36). Nor did He deny that He was "the Christ, the Son of the Blessed One" (Mark 14:61) but quietly accepted the title. In the face of such a statement, it is difficult to understand how hostile critics can suggest as they do that He never claimed deity for Himself. He always spoke and acted in a manner entirely consistent with such a claim.

Nothing could be more impressive than His total indifference to the insults and threats of His unscrupulous judges. For various reasons Pilate obviously desired to release Jesus, but He did nothing to make it easy for Pilate to do so or to assist him in this goal. He was certainly an unusual prisoner in this regard.

When Pilate suggested that he would listen favorably to Him, much to the governors' amazement, Jesus did not even try to answer. He showed not the slightest interest in Pilate's repeated endeavors to secure His release, whether by dissuading the Jews from pressing their demand or by persuading them to accept Barabbas the murderer instead of Jesus the Holy One.

When for the last time Pilate sought to release Jesus, he said, "Do you refuse to speak to me? . . . Don't you realize I have power either to free you or to crucify you?" (John 19:10). Jesus answered, "You would have no power over me if it were not given to you from above" (v. 11). Both by His silence and His words, Jesus made clear that it was Pilate and the Jews who were on trial before Him, and not He before them. *(31 Days)*

Aspects of the Atonement

The Atonement is moral in character, for it originates in and displays the glorious love of God, which is unselfish and totally free of self-seeking motives. This love, as manifested in the voluntary death of His only Son, is a moral stimulus to us and has broken the resistance of even the hardest of hearts (Hebrews 2:9; 1 John 4:9).

It is represented as a commercial transaction. It is a ransom paid to free people from the slavery of sin. In those passages that represent Christ's death as the price paid for our deliverance from sin and death, the Scriptures use the language of bargain and exchange (Matthew 20:28; 1 Timothy 2:6).

It has a legal significance, for Christ's death was an act of obedience to the law that sinning men had violated (Matthew 3:15; Galatians 4:4–5). It was a penalty borne in order to rescue the guilty from their merited punishment (Romans 4:25).

It is healing in its effects. In Scripture sin is frequently represented as a hereditary and contagious disease (Isaiah 1:3–6), for which Christ's atoning death provided the cure (Isaiah 53:5; 1 Peter 2:24). Jesus Himself presented His work in this manner (Matthew 9:12–13).

It is sacrificial in nature. The Atonement is described as a work of priestly mediation that reconciles man to God (Hebrews 9:11–12, 14, 22, 26). This is the consistent and prevailing conception throughout both Old and New Testaments. Hence, any view of the Atonement that does not provide a sufficient place for this aspect is inadequate.

It is popular in some theological circles to claim to have no theory of the Atonement. It is unnecessary, it is said, since it is the fact of the Atonement that saves, and not any theory about the fact. That sounds plausible, but it is frankly impossible. As Gresham Machen once said, one cannot believe with an empty head. One must have some comprehension of what was accomplished on the cross. The epistle to the Romans sets forth not only the fact but also the inner meaning of the Atonement. *(31 Days)*

Mysterious Darkness

"Darkness came over the whole land" (Luke 23:44). This was no ordinary darkness. God darkened the sun by His own means. It was not caused by an eclipse. The longest eclipse lasts but a few minutes, but this darkness continued for three hours. Again, it occurred during the Feast of the Passover, the time of full moon, when the moon was at its furthest from the sun.

This unique occurrence has historical support beyond the Bible. In Egypt, when Diogenes saw the darkness, with unconscious insight he exclaimed, "Either the Deity Himself suffers at this moment, or sympathizes with one that does."

In the second century Tertullian challenged his heathen adversaries with the following words, "At the moment of Christ's death, the light departed from the sun, and the land was darkened at noonday, which wonder is related in your own annals, and is preserved in your archives to this day."

This darkness was unique and symbolic. "The darkness was not caused by the absence of the sun, the occasion of our night," wrote W. R. Nicholson. "It was darkness at noon-time, a darkness in the presence of the sun, and while

313

the sun was uneclipsed by the intervention of another celestial body, a darkness we might say, which was the antagonist of light and the overcomer of it . . . The darkness of Calvary smothering the sun at noon! What an impressive thing! What a trembling conception of the almightiness of God!"

But why this darkness? It is because darkness and judgment go together. It assuredly was an awesome sign to the sign-seeking but Christ-rejecting Jews. It was an inspired commentary on the character and extent of His sufferings for us while He was being "stricken by God, smitten by him, and afflicted" (Isaiah 53:4). Peter, James, and John, intimates of Jesus, were admitted into the secrets of Gethsemane, but at Calvary God enveloped His Son's anguish in a darkness that concealed its full meaning. (*31 Days*)

Final Justice

Because of human sin, life on earth is clearly unjust. If God is as good and just as the Scriptures state and as we have maintained, how can He retain His character while permitting such a state of affairs to continue? If He remains inactive in this situation, it would appear that He is either uncaring or is powerless to correct and judge the many injustices of this life.

But both Scripture and history are filled with declarations that He is neither uncaring nor inactive. This life is not the end of all that there is. Such inequalities will be made right.

Where did Asaph discover the solution to his problem? He tells us, "Surely in vain have I kept my heart pure; in vain have I washed my hands in innocence . . .When I tried to understand all this, it was oppressive to me till I entered the sanctuary of God; then I understood their final destiny" (Psalm 73: 13, 16–17). Like him, we should take our perplexing problems into the presence of God and try to see things from His perspective. It is the end view that is important.

Scripture is filled with prophetic statements that a day is coming when injustices will be rectified and inequalities balanced out, when evil will be punished and virtue appropriately rewarded. This will take place at the day of judgment. Those who in this life have not availed themselves of the only way of salvation through the grace of God and the atoning death of Christ will not enter the gates of heaven. The Word is uncompromising: "Nothing impure will ever enter it, nor will anyone who does what is shameful or deceitful, but only those whose names are written in the Lamb's book of life" (Revelation 21:27). *(HB)*

The Time of His Coming

L U K E 2 1 : 3 1

he Bible tells us a sufficient amount to satisfy our faith, although not always enough to gratify our curiosity. The New Testament was not written to satisfy the inquisitive mind but to glorify the One who is coming again and to stimulate faith in Him. Although we may not know the exact day or hour, the Lord indicated that we could know when His coming was at hand. The coincidence of certain signs would be its sure precursor.

There would be a spiritual sign—widespread apostasy and departure from the faith (2 Thessalonians 2:3; 1 Timothy 4:1). Scoffers would ridicule the idea of His coming (2 Peter 3:3).

There would be political signs, days of peril nationally and socially (2 Timothy 3:1). "Nations will be in anguish and perplexity" (Luke 21:25).

There would be a financial sign—the great amassing of wealth. "You have hoarded wealth in the last days" (James 5:3).

There would be a Jewish sign. In the light of the astounding Six-Day War in June 1967 between Israel and the Arab world and the liberation of Jerusalem from the kind of external domination that had prevailed until then, our Lord's prediction is most significant. "Jerusalem will be trampled on by the Gentiles until the times of the Gentiles are fulfilled" (Luke 21:24). In the same discourse He referred to the budding of the fig tree—a symbol of the quickening into national life of Israel—and said, "When you see these things happening, you know that the kingdom of God is near" (Luke 21:31).

There would be an evangelistic sign. "And this gospel of the kingdom will be preached in the whole world as a testimony to all nations, and then the end will come" (Matthew 24:14). "The gospel must first be preached to all nations" (Mark 13:10). The great missionary activity of our day has resulted in Christianity's becoming for the first time a universal religion. There does not remain any major national group in which the church of Christ has not been established.

With the fulfillment of these signs so evidently before our eyes, we have abundant warrant for believing that "[He] is near, right at the door" (Mark 13:29). *(31 Days)*

Thankfulness

---

1 THESSALONIANS 5:18

Thanksgiving is not difficult when it flows from our recognition of the temporal and spiritual blessings that we consider desirable. But what of the burdens and disciplines and the sufferings and sorrows of life? Surely we cannot be expected to give thanks for those! But this is exactly what God does expect us to do. We are left with no option if we are His obedient children. We must be "always giving thanks to God the Father for everything, in the name of our Lord Jesus Christ" (Ephesians 5:20). These commands are devastatingly inclusive.

No one would suggest that this is always easy, but it is always possible, or God would not expect it of us. There is an Arab proverb that says, "All sunshine makes a desert," and it is true that if life were all joy and prosperity, unmixed with sorrow and adversity, our characters would be immeasurably poorer. Our loving Father knows the exact proportions in which to mix these ingredients, and we should thankfully and without question accept His dealings with us as the very best for us.

The correct response of the heart is expressed in *The Scottish Prayer Book:* "We praise Thee for the grace by which Thou dost enable us so to bear the ills of the pres-

319

ent world, that our souls are enriched by a fuller experience of Thy love, a more childlike dependence on Thy will, and a deeper sympathy with the suffering and the sad."

On his way to exile, John Chrysostom exclaimed, "Thank God for everything." Thanking God in one of his matchless letters, Samuel Rutherford wrote, "O, what I owe to the furnace, the file and the hammer of my Lord Jesus!"

A missionary was greatly discouraged. He knew that his work was not progressing as it should. One day, while visiting another missionary, he saw a motto card on the wall: *TRY THANKSGIVING!* It was an arrow to his soul. He suddenly realized that this element had been largely missing from his prayers.

There had been plenty of asking God for things he desired and needed; he had asked desperately at times but had forgotten to thank Him for what he received. He began to count his blessings and to pour out his heart in thanksgiving. *(PP)*

Pleading the Promises

"Every promise of Scripture is a writing of God," said Charles Haddon Spurgeon, "which may be pleaded before Him with this reasonable request, 'Do as Thou hast said.' The Creator will not cheat the creature who depends upon His truth; and far more, the heavenly Father will not break His word to His own child."

What is a promise? A promise is a written or verbal declaration that binds the person who makes it to perform a specified act. When applied to God, it is His pledge to do or refrain from doing a certain thing. Such promises form the basis of the prayer of faith. It is through prayer that these promises are turned into the facts and factors of one's Christian experience.

The validity and dependability of a promise rest on the character and resources of the one who makes it, just as the validity of a bank check depends on the integrity and bank balance of the one who signs it. The holy character and faithfulness of God make His promises credible. "He who promised is faithful," testified the writer of the letter to the Hebrews (10:23). "Not one word has failed of all His good promise," said the kneeling Solomon (1 Kings 8:56 NASB).

God's promises are thus bound up with His character and rest on four of His divine attributes: (1) His truth, which makes lying impossible; (2) His omniscience, which makes His being deceived or mistaken impossible; (3) His power, which makes everything possible; and (4) His unchangeableness, which precludes wavering or change.

So when we come to God armed with one of His promises, we can do so with the utmost confidence. We can share Abraham's unwavering trust. "With respect to the promise of God, he did not waver in unbelief, but grew strong in faith, giving glory to God, and being fully assured that what He had promised, He was able also to perform" (Romans 4:20–21 NASB). *(PP)*

Life in Heaven

Will we know one another in heaven? To many, this is the paramount question about life after death. Uncertainty as to the answer has dulled the desire of heaven for some. It would be no blissful place for them if they were unable to recognize friends and loved ones of the past. One of the anticipatory joys of heaven is the prospect of reunion. Our question has been expressed poignantly in verse by Robert Browning.

> When the holy angels meet us
> As we go to join their band,
> Shall we know the friends that greet us
> In the glorious spirit-land?

To that question J. H. Bavinck gives the following confident answer, an answer that has abundant support in Scripture: "The hope to see one another in heaven is entirely natural, genuinely human and in harmony with Scripture." Life in heaven will bring enrichment, not impoverishment. The author George MacDonald once posed the question in a humorous way, "Shall we be greater fools in Paradise than we are here?"

No Scripture passage suggests the abolition of all former relationships when we arrive in heaven. In a letter to Canon Barry, Sir William Robertson Nicoll, the noted religious editor, referring to the poet Robert Browning's views on this subject said:

"What I gathered from Browning . . . was that our personalities are distinct in the next world, and that a pure and holy love between individuals in this life is a creation of God, and will live on in the next."

It is the essential element of personality that will persist after death, not the temporary "tent" in which it is housed on this earth. The body is destined to return to dust, but the inward man, the spirit, lives on, and its identity with the body is not breached.

Angels have no bodies, and yet they exist and act as distinct personalities. If angels who have no bodies are able to recognize one another, why should this not be possible for believers? In Daniel 9:21 and 10:13 it is recorded that Michael the archangel came to the assistance of his colleague Gabriel when the latter was hindered in his mission by satanic beings. If angels, why not men and women? *(HB)*

Should We Fast?

It is noteworthy that although our Lord fasted at times, as during the temptation in the wilderness (Matthew 4:2), and although He instructed His disciples as to the spirit in which fasting is to be undertaken (Matthew 6:16–18), He refrained from appointing any fast as an ordinance of His kingdom (Matthew 9:14–17; 11:18–19). While not disapproving of or abolishing the practice of fasting, Jesus lifted it out of the straitjacket of old covenant legalism into the liberty of the new covenant.

Jesus Himself doubtless observed all the prescribed Jewish fasts, but in all His teaching He spoke of fasting only twice. Indeed, so little an ascetic was He in His lifestyle that they laid the charge against Him—utterly unfounded—of being a glutton and a drunkard. Nowhere did He make fasting obligatory.

When the disciples of John asked Jesus, "Why do we and the Pharisees fast, but Your disciples do not fast?" (Matthew 9:14 NASB), His reply was that since fasting was a sign of mourning, it would be inappropriate to engage in it while He as Messiah and Bridegroom was with them (Matthew 9:14–17). The time would come when He would be removed from them. Then it would not be inconsistent to fast. But it should be noted that He left the question open. (Textual scholars consider *fasting* in Matthew 17:21 and Mark 9:29 [KJV] to be added to the text by scribes at a later time.)

There are only four indisputable references to voluntary fasting in the New Testament. In addition to the two that have been cited, there are two in the book of Acts—13:2 and 14:23. The references in 2 Corinthians 6:5 and 11:27 seem to have involuntary fasting in view.

In a penetrating study of the subject of voluntary fasting, Dr. Henry W. Frost asserts that it is nowhere placed on the Christian as a duty. We may or may not fast, as we choose. David Livingstone had very definite views on the subject. "Fasting and vigils without a special object in view are time run to waste. They are made to minister to a sort of self-gratification instead of being turned to good account." *(PP)*

Redeem the Time

When Paul urged the Ephesian Christians to redeem the time (Ephesians 5:16), he was implying that there is a sense in which time is to be bought. It becomes ours by purchase and exchange. There is a price, and sometimes a high price, to be paid for its best use.

Henry Martyn of India was a man unusually successful in the art of redeeming the time, or "buying up opportunities," as Henry Alford has put it. So urgent did he deem his translation work that he found it impossible to waste an hour. The vision of nations was always before his eyes, waiting for the truth that lay locked up in the Book he was translating. To him, the need of a lost part of the world proved an impelling motive to redeem the hours, and in the brief six years of his meteoric missionary career, he translated the New Testament into three languages.

One practical step that can be taken to secure adequate time for prayer is to plug the leaks. We should not think of our day in terms only of hours, but in smaller portions of time, and aim to make constructive use of each of these. Dr. F. B. Meyer, noted preacher and author, packed more into his life than most of his contemporaries. And his secret? It was said of him that, like John Wesley, he divided his life into periods of five minutes and then endeavored to make each period count for God.

The secret of prodigious achievements, it is said, lay in knowing the difference between ten minutes and a quarter of an hour. How many periods of five, ten, or fifteen minutes that could be devoted to prayer do we waste or leave unemployed in the course of a day? Let us determine to make more and better use of these uncommitted but potentially valuable minutes. *(PP)*

———

Rewards in Heaven

he whole subject of rewards for the believer in heaven is one that is rarely thought of by the ordinary Christian, or even by the student of the Scriptures. It is at once both a joyous and a solemn theme, and should serve as a potent incentive for holiness of life." So wrote Wilbur M. Smith many years ago, and circumstances have changed little since then with regard to this topic.

There are spiritual teachers who regard the whole concept of rewards for service as a very second-rate motivation. They liken it to bribing a child with candy for good behavior. But Jesus in no way offered support to this viewpoint. The apostle Paul also teaches about rewards in several of his letters.

It goes without saying that no acts of merit of ours can win salvation, for that is a result of God's incredible and unmerited love. But the very fact that Jesus spoke of rewards for service on a number of occasions would indicate that He considered their granting an important article of faith. But in no way did He suggest or imply that service was a method of accumulating merit and thereby receiving salvation. Eternal life is a gift, not a reward.

The language in which the concept of rewards is clothed is highly symbolic and should be interpreted accordingly. Of course, faithful service brings rewards in this life as well as in the life to come. Both are mentioned in the following verse: "'I tell you the truth,' Jesus said to them, 'no one who has left home or wife or brothers or parents or children for the sake of the kingdom of God will fail to receive many times as much in this age and, in the age to come, eternal life'" (Luke 18:29). *(HB)*

Prayer and Revival

*S*ome years ago a great revival swept over Korea, the fruits of which remain to the present day. This revival had been prayed down. Four missionaries of different denominations had agreed to meet together to pray daily at noon. At the end of one month a brother proposed that "as nothing had happened," the prayer meetings should be discontinued. "Let us each pray at home as we find it convenient," he said. The others, however, protested that they ought rather to spend even more time in prayer each day. So they continued the daily prayer meetings for four months. Then suddenly the blessing began to be poured out.

In *Evangelical Christian* magazine, one of the missionaries declared: "It paid well to have spent several months in prayer; for when God gave the Holy Spirit, He accomplished more in half a day than all the missionaries together could have accomplished in half a year." In less than two months more than two thousand souls were converted. In one church it was announced that a daily prayer meeting would be held every morning at 4:30. The very first day four hundred people arrived long before the stated hour, eager to pray. The number rapidly increased to six hundred. Unbelieving people came to see what was happening. They exclaimed in astonishment, "The living God is among you!"

When God plans to send revival blessing, He lays a burden for it on the hearts of those who make themselves available to Him. An aged saint came to his pastor one night and said, "We are about to have a revival." He was asked how he knew so. His answer was, "I went into the stable to take care of my cattle two hours ago, and there the Lord has kept me in prayer until just now. And I feel we are going to be revived." It proved to be the beginning of a revival. Are we similarly available? *(PP)*

Life Is a Tapestry

GENESIS 50:20

The experiences of life when taken in isolation may seem anything but good, but blended together the result is only good.

In adverse circumstances unbelief asks, "How can this be working for good?" The answer is, "Wait until the Great Physician has finished writing the prescription." Who cannot look back on life to see that things considered disastrous proved in the ultimate to be blessings in disguise? An artist blends colors that to the unskilled eye seem far removed from the objective. But wait until she has finished her mixing.

Life has been likened to an elaborate tapestry being woven on the loom. For the beauty of the pattern it is imperative that the colors must not be all of the same hue. Some must be bright and beautiful, others dark and somber. It is as they are all worked together that they contribute to the beauty of the pattern.

In time of severe trial there is always the temptation, while assenting to the truth in general, to feel that our present circumstances are an exception. If that were so, the text is untrue, and the truth of the overruling providence of God in the affairs of humanity has no meaning.

As tragedy upon tragedy overwhelmed Joseph—banishment from home, sale as a slave, unjust imprisonment—it was difficult for him to see these untoward events working together for his good. Yet in retrospect he said to his brothers, "But as for you, ye thought evil against me; but God meant it unto good" (Genesis 50:20 KJV).

In the events of life God has an end in view that is worthy of Him and will bring about our fullest praise and thanksgiving when we cease to know in part. Even if called upon to face the wrath of humans or Devil, we can confidently rest in the assurance that it will ultimately result in praise to God, and that which cannot do so will be restrained. *(SM)*

Greater Fruitfulness

The loving heavenly Father can be trusted in the adaptation, timing, and duration of the discipline His love permits. We are safe in His hands.

The discipline is always preparatory to blessing and can bring nothing but blessing when rightly received. It is here that our responsibility lies. Food not digested is a discomfort, not a blessing. Disciplines not rightly received sour rather than sweeten the character. To ask "Why?" when the chastening stroke falls is in effect to charge the all-wise and all-loving God with being harsh. He does not rend the heart merely to demonstrate His power and sovereignty but to prepare us for greater fruitfulness. He prunes every branch that does bear fruit to increase its yield. The discipline is lovingly purposeful. How do we react to God's plow? Does it soften, subdue, or chasten us? Or does it harden and stiffen our resistance to His will? Does it sweeten or sour us?

Our reaction to family problems and financial reverses, to suffering and disappointment, to thwarted ambitions and disappointed expectations is all-important. If we submit, feeling that resistance is counterproductive, that is better than continued rebellion. If we respond to God's dealings glumly, that is still attaining higher ground. But it is when we embrace God's unexplained difficult providences with a song that God is most glorified and we are most blessed. When Samuel Rutherford lay in Aberdeen prison, he used to write at the top of his letters, "God's Palace, Aberdeen."

Madame Guyon, a cultured Frenchwoman, was imprisoned for her faith from 1695 to 1705. Instead of complaining at her lot, she joyously accepted God's will as her gift from Him. "While I was a prisoner in Vincennes," she wrote, "I passed my time in great peace. I sang songs of joy which the maid who served me learned by heart as fast as I made them. And we together sang Thy praises, O my God. The stones of my prison walls shone like rubies in my eyes. My heart was full of that joy which Thou givest to them that love Thee in the midst of their greatest crosses." *(SM)*

He Is Worthy

We are by nature essentially selfish beings. And even after we have been made partakers of the divine nature, so strong is the power of the old life that we are usually more interested in receiving than in giving. Was not our Lord's statement, "It is more blessed to give than to receive" (Acts 20:35), a tacit correction of this tendency? In our relationship with God we are constantly at the receiving end. We commence our Christian life by receiving the atonement (Romans 5:11). We continue our Christian life by receiving the abundance of grace (Romans 5:17). We conclude our Christian life by being received into glory (1 Timothy 3:16). We are constantly tugging at God's skirts for some desired blessing, and He delights to have it so, but we forget that He too yearns to receive from us what we alone can give Him.

In one sense we cannot enrich Christ. But nothing is more heartening to Him than the spontaneous voicing of our appreciation of His intrinsic worth, and nothing is more enriching to ourselves, for it is in the process of being worshiped that God communicates His presence to people.

Writing in this connection, C. S. Lewis says,

> To see what the doctrine really means, we must suppose ourselves to be in perfect love with God—drunk with, drowned in, dissolved by that delight which, far from remaining pent up within ourselves as incommunicable, hence hardly tolerable bliss, flows out from us incessantly again in effortless and perfect expression, our joy no more separable from the praise in which it liberates and utters itself than the brightness of a mirror is separable from the brightness it sheds. The Scottish catechism says that man's chief end is "to glorify God and to enjoy Him forever." But we shall then know that these are the same thing. Fully to enjoy is to glorify. In commanding us to glorify Him, God is inviting us to enjoy Him. *(SM)*

―――――⚬―――――

The Wick's Oil

In Old Testament times one of the functions of the priests was to remove with golden snuffers the encrustation from the wick; otherwise, there would have been no clear shining. Sometimes our High Priest must use the golden snuffers to remove from our lives things that encrust and hinder the clear shining of the light. He performs this office through His Word applied in power to the heart by the Holy Spirit. Let us cherish this ministry, painful though it be.

It is by the dynamic of the Spirit alone that the church can fulfill its function, not by resources of intellect or finance or zeal. Propaganda, organization, and brilliance are no substitute for the Holy Ghost. New techniques and better methods have their place, but they do not dispense with the need for the dynamic of the Spirit. We will see success in our missionary work only when He has prepared the way for our coming. Where missions have flourished, there is evidence of the Spirit having been at work before the advent of the missionary, producing heart-hunger, creating expectation, causing disillusionment with their religions and persuading of the insufficiency of the light they had.

What is implied in the phrase "but by my Spirit" (Zechariah 4:6 KJV)? This phrase means that in all Christian work the superhuman factor is of supreme importance. True, it operates through the human, but it is the human interpenetrated by the Divine as the wick is saturated with the oil, which is the Holy Spirit. Then we will not rely on our argument or persuasion to win converts and build up believers in their faith. We will trust Him to manipulate circumstances and overcome obstacles in our path. We will expect Him to enable us to finish the work.

What a privilege is ours—to have the flame of God consume us as we bring light to a world enveloped in midnight darkness! On reaching the shores of India, Henry Martyn said, "And now, let me burn out for God." He did—in six short years, but with an incredible legacy of achievement in Bible translation left behind him. *(SM)*

God Controls Circumstances

*P*otentates and politicians may pride themselves that they are making history and may create great libraries to perpetuate their achievements. But Paul cuts them down to size when he writes, "He [God] fixed the epochs of their history and the limits of their territory" (Acts 17:26 NEB). As sovereign Lord of the universe, He controls the circumstances and orders them as He will. And His will is good. "Moreover we know that to those who love God . . . everything that happens fits into a pattern for good" (Romans 8:28 PHILLIPS).

When God declared, "O house of Israel, can I not do with you as this potter does? . . . Like clay in the hand of the potter, so are you in my hand, O house of Israel" (Jeremiah 18:6), He was expressing His absolute control of events and circumstances.

No circumstance comes to pass by chance, although its significance may not be apparent at the time. Later it may be seen as a vital factor in the unfolding of a life plan. This was so in my life.

As a young man, I applied for admission to the Bible Institute of Los Angeles and asked them to send the appropriate forms. In due course I received a reply from the registrar saying that he was sending the material under separate cover, but it never arrived. At the time I wrote that letter, I did not know that a Bible college had been founded recently in New Zealand. In the waiting period, I met some of its students, who encouraged me to enroll there. In the providence of God, I later became principal of the Bible College of New Zealand for a number of years. God had overruled an office glitch in Los Angeles to direct me into His plan for my life.

The lesson is that when we trustfully commit our way to the Lord as we are urged to do (Psalm 37:5), we can confidently expect Him to order the circumstances and to guide us to opportunities that are in line with His plan. *(EL)*

Steps in Discerning God's Will

Be unconditionally willing to do it, whatever it is. It may be that your will needs to be redirected. Be willing to be made willing.

- Be obedient to any light the Lord has already given. If you are not obeying that, why expect more?

- Be patient. The road ahead may not be revealed all at once; it seldom is. But God will show you each step as you need to take it. We sing the hymn "One Step Enough for Me" but don't always mean it.

- Remember the intellectual component in this exercise. John Wesley maintained, "God generally guides me by presenting reasons to my mind for acting in a certain way"—not feelings to my heart.

- Gather all the information you can about the options that are open to you.

- Seek advice from your Christian parents, your pastor, or a trusted Christian counselor. However, don't allow them to make the decision for you. It is your life that is at stake, and you will have to live with the consequences of that decision.

- Ensure that the course you propose to pursue is biblically legitimate. Submit it to the test of Scripture.

- List the pros and cons of the course you propose, and as you weigh them, ask the Holy Spirit to sway your mind in the direction of His will, believing that He does it in keeping with James 1:5.

- Don't ask for extraordinary guidance, for that is the exception and not the rule, especially as you mature spiritually. Spectacular signs are given only by the sovereign choice of God. Faith is content with quiet guidance.

- Make the best decision you can in light of the facts, believing God has answered your prayer for wisdom.

- Expect the witness of the Spirit in a deepening conviction that this is the will of God for you. Circumstances may confirm your guidance. (F.I.)

The Lamb's Book of Life

hat does it mean to have one's name written in the Lamb's Book of Life?

Concerning the judgment in front of the great white throne we read, "Then I saw a great white throne . . . And I saw the dead, great and small, standing before the throne, and books were opened. Another book was opened, which is the book of life. The dead were judged according to what they had done as recorded in the books" (Revelation 20:11–12).

One set of books, then, contains the record of each person's life history. The other book is the Lamb's Book of Life. The first record can bring only condemnation, for all have fallen short of God's standards. In the Book of Life are recorded the names of those who have repented of their sins and exercised saving faith in Christ as Redeemer and Savior.

John Bunyan, in his *Pilgrim's Progress,* describes the armed man who came up to the table where the man with the book and the inkhorn was seated and said, "Set down my name." It is open to anyone to do just that. A living faith in Christ, the Lamb of God who "takes away the sin of the world," is the sole condition for having our names written in that book, and that constitutes our passport through the pearly gates. "They that trust in Jesus Christ," writes Alexander Maclaren, "shall have their names written in the Book of Life; graven on the High Priest's breastplate, and inscribed on His mighty hand and His faithful heart."

Why not make absolutely certain of heaven by opening your heart to Christ the Savior and Lord right now, inviting Him to enter, to cleanse it from sin, and to make it His permanent dwelling-place? *(HB)*

Note to the Reader

The publisher invites you to share your response to the message of this book by writing Discovery House Publishers, P.O. Box 3566, Grand Rapids, MI 49501, U.S.A. For information about other Discovery House books, music, videos, or DVDs, contact us at the same address or call 1-800-653-8333. Find us on the Internet at http://www.dhp.org/ or send e-mail to books@dhp.org.